S0-BYA-200

POCKET LIBRARY OF "STUDIES" IN ART

XXV

EDWARD G. CLARE

ST. NICHOLAS
HIS LEGENDS AND ICONOGRAPHY

LEO S. OLSCHKI EDITORE

FIRENZE

MCMLXXXV

Publication of this work has been made possible by a grant from the Ludwig Vogelstein Foundation, Inc., Douglas Blair Turnbaugh, Treasurer, in memory of Jane Sebarsky, 1911-1983, a devoted member of its board of directors.

ISBN 88 222 3330 1

to ULLA

ACKNOWLEDGEMENTS

In the course of this study I received cooperation from many individuals and institutions, and I would like to mention some who have proven most important in bringing this book to publication. Foremost among those who were of considerable help to me is my wife Ulla. The dedication in her name is but a small gesture of appreciation for her tireless assistance and for lending her translating, editing and typing skills to the benefit of this work. The idea to research the iconography of St. Nicholas from his origin in Byzantium to the modern Santa Claus was suggested to me by Professor Mirella D'Ancona of Hunter College, City University of New York, and I am deeply grateful for her suggestions and corrections throughout the writing of the manuscript.

This work would have remained in manuscript form had it not been for the generous grant from the Ludwig Vogelstein Foundation, and I am particularly thankful for the support of the Foundation's treasurer, Mr. Douglas Turnbaugh. Finally, I appreciate the willingness of Dr. Alessandro Olschki to take the risk inherent in publishing an unknown author.

New York, April 1984

INTRODUCTORY NOTE

The cult of Saint Nicholas has endured almost as long as Christianity. It began in the early centuries after Christ and continues to the present day. Nicholas remains the only saint who is important and popular in the Roman Catholic as well as in the Orthodox Eastern Church. He is also highly respected among Protestants, and in his modern guise as Santa Claus he is admired by everyone, even the non-religious person. In short, he is loved wherever European culture exists.

This work is a study of the origin of St. Nicholas in Byzantium and the expansion of his cult far beyond that sphere. It is not an attempt to present an encyclopedic collection of art representing St. Nicholas. Nevertheless, an effort has been made to demonstrate the great geographic diversity, continuity, adaptability, and popularity of the subject throughout the centuries. The study's main thrust is directed toward the saint's changing iconography in art and a better understanding of his historical position in our culture.

Part One

SAINT NICHOLAS IN BYZANTIUM

The Origin of His Cult

Saint Nicholas was born in the city of Patras at an unknown date. While still a young man, he became the bishop of Myra, the town in which he also died, after a devout and eventful life, in 343 A.D.[1] During his lifetime, as well as after his death, he was credited with many miracles which left a lasting imprint on the minds of successive generations. Legends reveal St. Nicholas not only as a most versatile patron of young women, boys, bankers, sailors and thieves, but also as a source of influence on the great emperor Constantine. As bishop of Myra, Nicholas represented the center of the entire community, and his presence was felt from birth to death. His life, full of care for his people and of intercessions with his superhuman and supernatural powers for the good of mankind, became

---

[1] Jacobus de Voragine, *The Golden Legend*, trans. Granger Ryan and Helmut Ripperger, New York, Arno Press 1969, p. 21.

a worthy theme for art and literature, and it must have been the popularity of his deeds which led to the spread of his cult from Myra to the rest of Byzantium and to the world beyond. Indeed, the legends attributed to Nicholas gave him the status of a god.

When Nicholas became bishop of Myra, the Greek goddess Artemis still constituted a powerful religious force in this town; her temple there was regarded as the most beautiful in Lycia.[2] In the Artemis legend,[3] Nicholas is credited with the destruction of this temple,[4] and the defeat of the pagan goddess must have affirmed and enhanced his Christian leadership. The fact that Constantine only permitted Christian churches in his new capital in the fourth century undoubtedly helped the triumph of Christianity in Myra as well. In the inevitable clash between the two competing religions, the local bishop would have been the recipient of Christian praise, and since Nicholas was the spiritual leader at the time of the Christian ascendancy in Myra, he could be considered the successor of Artemis in this city.

Earliest evidence of an existing St. Nicholas cult appears in a text written in 565 A.D. on the life of Saint

---

[2] Gustav Anrich, *Hagios Nikolaos, der heilige Nikolaos in der griechischen Kirche*, 2 vols., Leipzig, B. G. Teubner 1913-17, 2: 505.

[3] Anrich, 2: 433-434. Anrich traces the Artemis legend through the tenth century text of Metaphrates back to the ninth century. He discusses the sources of all Greek St. Nicholas legends in great detail in his outstanding study based on the oldest manuscripts.

[4] Jacobus., p. 19. *The Golden Legend* refers to a tree consecrated to Diana which was cut down by St. Nicholas.

Nicholas of Sion.[5] It is mentioned here that a famous Nicholas church, believed by the German scholar Gustav Anrich to date before 530, was built over the tomb of Nicholas near the town of Myra.[6] Since the church was already well known in 565, we may assume that his cult was firmly established locally before this date. Of importance is also that the church was built over his tomb, indicating that it might have been a pilgrim church. The same document reports the meeting of the synod of Lycian bishops in Myra on the feast day of St. Nicholas, December 6, and additional proof of his emerging cult lies in the increased usage of his name: before the fourth century the name was rare, but after that time it became better known, especially in Lycia.[7]

During the Justinian era (527-565) the cult expanded to other areas beyond Lycia. Perhaps the first church dedicated to Nicholas outside Lycia was the one built in Constantinople at latest in the first half of the sixth century. In a manuscript by Prokop, written c 560,[8] it was referred to as the « Hieron on the Golden Horn ».

---

[5] ANRICH, 2: 449.

[6] ANRICH, 2: 449. « Die um 565 verfasste Vita Nicolai Sionitae setzt das Bestehen des Nicholaomartyrion für spätestens um 530 voraus ... Angaben über die mit einer Bischofssynode verbundenen Rosalien lassen darauf schliessen ... dass wenigstens in Myra Nikolaos bereits ein bedeutender Heiliger ist, dessen Kult darum wohl weiter in die Vergangenheit zurückreicht ».

[7] *Ibid.*, 2: 452.

[8] *Ibid.*, 2: 459. « Da Prokops Werk über die Bauten Justinians um 560 verfasst, muss das Hieron am Goldenen Horn spätestens um die Mitte des 6. Jahrhunderts gebaut worden sein: das erste Erscheinen unseres Heiligen auf der Bühne der grossen Welt ».

We also find the oldest text of a Nicholas legend originating during the reign of Justinian.[9] The manuscript, *Praxis de stratelatis*, recounts the story of the first and foremost legend in Byzantium. The events take place in the lifetime of Constantine the Great, when three Byzantine generals, Herpylion, Nepotianus and Ursus, witnessed St. Nicholas as he saved three innocent men from execution. A similar predicament befell the three generals upon their return to Constantinople when they were wrongfully thrown into prison. Remembering St. Nicholas, they prayed to him for help. That very night he appeared to Constantine in a dream and demanded that the emperor should pardon the three guiltless commanders. The next day Constantine set them free, and gratefully the three liberated men returned to Myra to pay their respects to the saint and to present gifts from the emperor.

It is known that a Flavius Nepotianus was consul in 336 and that a Flavius Ursus held the same office in 338.[10] These historical facts as well as the status of Emperor Constantine lend authenticity to the story and provide a possible explanation for the legend's importance and its frequent appearance in the East.[11] Moreover, in this age

---

[9] ANRICH, 2: 369-377. See these pages for a full investigation of the date; the extreme dates being between the years 460 to 580.

P. 370. « So ergäben sich etwa die Jahre 460 und 580 als äusserste Grenzen nach oben und unten ».

[10] ANRICH, 2: 371. « Auch die Namen des ersten und zweiten der Stratelaten sind historisch. Ein Flavius Nepotianus ist 336, ein Flavius Ursus 338 Konsul gewesen ».

[11] *Ibid.*, 2: 30. « Diese berühmteste Praxis des Nikolaus ist – noch ganz abgesehen von ihrer Einarbeitung in die Nikolausviten – in über 50 Hss. auf uns gekommen. Die grosse Mehrzahl derselben

dreams, and their religious interpretation, were of some consequence. Therefore, perhaps the dramatic dream sequence between Nicholas and Constantine held particular sway in the capital of the Empire and gave Nicholas' reputation the prestige that attracted the early writers who immortalised his legends.

Little evidence points to any further growth of the cult during the seventh and eighth century. This, of course, could be the result of the iconoclast controversy during this era when few cultural achievements occurred throughout the Byzantine Empire.

But the ninth century marks the full bloom and evolution of Nicholas' cult in Byzantium. His name is now found in abundance outside Lycia,[12] and it was in these years that Nicholas grew to a dominant figure in holy literature. The first comprehensive vita of St. Nicholas, written by Michael the Archimandrite in the early ninth century,[13] included the following legends of his wondrous deeds:

1. *Praxis de stratelatis*; the story of the three Byzantine generals who were saved by St. Nicholas from execution;

---

stellt einen einheitlichen Typus dar, dessen Text nur in, wenn auch zahlreichen, so doch verhältnismässig belanglosen Einzelheiten variiert ». See also p. 461.

[12] *Ibid.*, 2: 460.

[13] ANRICH, 2: 276. « Die Vita per Michaelen ist nächst der Praxis de Stratelatis der bedeutendste Text über Nikolaus von Myra. Denn sie ist die kanonische Lebensbeschreibung des Heiligen geblieben ... und durch die Metaphrastische Vita ist für alle Zeiten die Grundlage der Nikolauslegende geblieben ».

1: 111. The Vita by Michael is reproduced here in the original Greek.

2: 261. Here the stories are discussed in German.

2. *Praxis de tribus filiabus*; Nicholas secretly gives three bags of gold for three destitute maidens;

3. *Praxis de nautis*; the saint saves seamen in a storm;

4. *Praxis de navibus frumentariis in portu*; St. Nicholas procures grain from some grain ships in port in order to save his famine-stricken diocese;

5. *Thauma de Artemide*; he warns pilgrims going to his tomb to throw away the dangerous oil they were given by Artemis, who had disguised herself as a nun.

Details of these stories will emerge later in this work when we study the iconography of the saint in Italian painting.

Throughout the ninth century, Nicholas' life served as the subject for laudatory speeches by leading religious figures. Before 826, Joseph the Hymnograph and Theodorus the Studite composed what is believed to be the oldest hymn to the saint.[14] Later in the century, in 880, another, most significant development of the cult took place when Johannes Diaconus of Naples wrote the first Latin biography of Nicholas based on Greek texts.[15] And in the following year, on May 1, 881, a great church built by Emperor Basil I was dedicated to the Theotokos, the archangel Michael, the prophet Elias, and to St. Nicholas.[16]

It was in the tenth century that Simeon Metaphrastes produced the last classical Greek text on the life of Nicholas.[17] This vita by Metaphrastes is considered to be a

---

[14] *Ibid.*, 2: 463.
[15] *Ibid.*, 2: 477.
[16] *Ibid.*, 2: 465.
[17] *Ibid.*, 2: 468.

revision and expansion of Michael and provides the foundation for future biographies of the saint.[18] By now Nicholas' cult had gained its full maturity in Byzantium, and from the tenth century on people, villages, churches, and monasteries were named after the bishop of Myra:[19] according to the Ceremonial Book by Konstantinos Porphyrogenitos (912-59), an asylum called the Hagios Nicholaos existed as part of the Hagia Sophia;[20] Empress Irene had constructed a church dedicated to Nicholas in 1118;[21] in 1200 Antonios of Novgorod mentioned a St. Nicholas church near the middle of the northeast wall at the Golden Horn, and another church, built on the slope of the acropolis in Constantinople;[22] finally, Alexander, a Russian pilgrim, gave a description of a convent called Hagios Nikolas in his Pilgrim Book, written in 1393.[23]

In addition to these early Greek churches, Constantinople also possessed Latin churches consecrated to the saint. This is not surprising if we remember that it was the eastern center of trade and that Nicholas had become the patron of seamen. Thus a St. Nicholas church, built for the traders of Pisa, was cited in 1192,[24] and a report of 1267 confirmed the existence of a Venetian St. Nicholas church located in the Galata, opposite the Golden Horn.[25]

---

[18] *Ibid.*, 2: 276. See the German quote in note 13 above.
[19] *Ibid.*, 2: 468.
[20] *Ibid.*, 2: 469.
[21] *Ibid.*, 2: 470.
[22] *Ibid.*, 2: 471.
[23] *Ibid.*, 2: 471.
[24] *Ibid.*, 2: 472.
[25] *Ibid.*, 2: 472.

No doubt, the cult of Nicholas reached its peak in Constantinople, then radiated to other centers in the Orthodox East. The Orthodox Christians of Syria, Palestine and Egypt, for example, practiced a language and religion common to Constantinople, and while Nicholas was still considered a foreign saint in the eighth century calendar of Jerusalem, he had attained a secure place in the liturgy of this holy city by the twelfth century.[26] Nearby Bethlehem, the birthplace of Christ, possessed an active St. Nicholas church in the eleventh century, and the name itself, Nicholas, had become quite a favorite in these regions: we even find one orthodox Patriarch Nicholas of Antioch in the ninth and two more in the thirteenth century; and a hundred years later, a Nicholas was Patriarch of Alexandria, Egypt.[27]

Based on the documented evidence presented by Gustav Anrich, it is apparent that Constantinople had become the focal point of the St. Nicholas cult outside Myra, and since the capital acted as a pivot between East and West, its influences were felt in many distant corners of the world. It was just natural, therefore, that the cult of Nicholas – once it had reached the shores of the Bosporus – would receive the necessary impulse to be propelled to the rest of Europe. Constantinople's culture travelled easily to Italy and western Europe through Sicily and Calabria which had both been politically associated with the Byzantine Empire, and the Balkan countries were no less receptive to the concepts and ideologies of Byzantine civilization, especially after their conversion to the Orthodox faith. Further to

[26] *Ibid.*, 2: 473.
[27] *Ibid.*, 2: 474.

the north, trade contacts exposed Russia first to the culture, then to the religion of Byzantium; an introduction, which carried as one of its results the eventual acknowledgment of St. Nicholas as her official patron. And while it is quite likely that the cult was mainly nourished through Byzantine literature, art and the Orthodox Church, the generally felt compassion of Nicholas for his fellow men in time of need surely must have played a major role in the enthusiastic, universal reception and acceptance of the saint.

The Iconography of Saint Nicholas in the Orthodox Church

In discussing the iconography of St. Nicholas in the Eastern Church, I shall only refer to icon painting. The icon is not only a beautiful art object, it also holds a special place in the Orthodox Church: regarded as a representative of the holy figure painted on the panel, it should be treated as if that person were alive. Honor given to the icon is honor given to the saint in person. Such reverence may be offered in the form of placing burning candles at the icon or by prostrating before the image; earliest reference to proskynesis, the act of prostration before an icon, is given by Hypatius of Ephesus in the first half of the sixth century.[28] Within the early church, icons served as wall decoration, and from about the tenth

[28] Kurt Weitzmann, et al. *A Treasury of Icons from the Sinai Peninsula, Greece, Bulgaria and Yugoslavia*, New York, Harry N. Abrams 1966, p. 2.

century on they occupied a position on the iconostasis, a wooden lacework which separates the altar from the congregation.[29] It was the small size of many icons which permitted their use at home as well as in the church. This very portability, and the particularly attractive nature of the icon, would make it an integral part of the development of St. Nicholas' cult.

The first icons date from the fourth century. Production over the next hundred years increased to a notable degree, and by the sixth century the icon cult was well established in the Byzantine Empire.[30] Early icon painting employed encaustic and tempera techniques, but since no icon in the encaustic manner can be dated later than the eighth century, it appears that tempera was the only technique engaged after that period.[31] This antique method of panel painting was preserved in Byzantium and transmitted by its artists to the West.[32] In all likelihood, the idea of icons as representatives of dead saints came from Egypt, where it derived from the usage of painting portraits on wood for burial rites. Surviving portrait panels from the second and third century, which had been placed on top of mummies, at least lend support to this theory.[33] The

---

[29] *Ibid.*, p. 9.

[30] Kurt Weitzmann, *The Monastery of Saint Catherine at Mount Sinai: The Icons*, vol. 1: *From the Sixth to the Tenth Century*, New Jersey, Princeton, Princeton University Press 1976, p. 5.

[31] *Ibid.*, p. 9.

[32] Otto Demus, *Byzantine Art and the West*, New York, New York University Press 1970, p. 205.

[33] H. P. Gerhard, *The World of Icons*, New York, Harper and Row 1971, p. 47.

encaustic technique and spiritual style of these paintings seem to have found their continuance in icon painting.

Enhancing the special quality and importance of icons are the miracles which are attributed to many of them. For example, the Kazankaya Mother of God icon, dating from the sixteenth century, had nine copies included in the Festival Calendar of the Russian Orthodox Church as miracle-working icons.[34] Other icons were copied not only for their miraculous aspect but also for their exceptional beauty or because they were painted by a great master. This multiplicity of similar icons painted in different periods creates, of course, a problem in the process of icon-dating. Furthermore, only few icons have outlasted the early centuries. In the course of the iconoclastic period (726-843) most icons from the preceding centuries were destroyed, their production and worship discontinued within Byzantium. After 843, however, icons were restored to their place of honor, and workshops which had resorted to the painting of animal and garden scenes now resumed religious panel painting. Yet even greater destruction was to come centuries later in 1204, when the Fourth Crusade sacked Constantinople and burnt it to the ground. According to Otto Demus, less than 1 % of the total Byzantine art production survived the Crusade.[35]

Fortunately, some of the oldest and best icons managed to endure these destructive events in the remote monastery of St. Catherine at Mount Sinai in present-day Egypt. The shrewd monks of St. Catherine were able to save their

---

[34] *Ibid.*, p. 212.

[35] DEMUS, p. 3.

monastery during the seventh and eighth century from the Arab conquerors by producing a document giving them protection, sealed by the Prophet Mahomet.[36] Although probably a forgery, it did rescue the monastery and its religious art. St. Catherine was now safe in Moslem territory, isolated from the iconoclasm that raged in the rest of Byzantium. I would like to begin our pilgrimage through art by looking at some early St. Nicholas images located here in St. Catherine.

The oldest remaining painting of Nicholas in Byzantium is believed to be either from the monastic art of Egypt or from the Palestinian school of the seventh or eighth century.[37] In this extremely rare panel painting, which represents the only extant pre-iconoclastic St. Nicholas, he shares a diptych with St. Paul, St. Peter, and St. John Chrysostom (Fig. 1). The most conspicuous aspects of the saint's image in the pre-iconoclastic style lie in his large eyes, the long, white beard, and the lobate crosses on his omophorion. The icon depicts Nicholas full-length, bottom left, carrying the Gospels in his clearly visible left hand while the right hand is raised in blessing. A classical influence can be detected in the drapery and his slight *contrapposto.* Altogether,

---

[36] GERHARD, p. 74.

[37] M. and G. SOTIRIOU, *Icones du Mont Sinai*, 2 vols. (Athènes, Collection de l'Institut Français d'Athènes, 1956-58), 2: 237. « Les icones 20 et 21 [our Fig. 1] sont apparentées aux fresques coptes de Baouit et nous donnent une idée de la spiritualité, de la puissance d'expression des images monastiques en Egypte autour du VIIe-VIIIe siècles ».

WEITZMANN, *The Monastery of St. Catherine*, pp. 58-59. Weitzmann agrees with Sotiriou on the date but believes that the icon may come from Palestine.

Fig. 1. - Mount Sinai, Monastery of St. Catherine: *St. Paul, St. Peter, St. Nicholas, and St. Chrysostom.* Diptych icon, 7th or 8th century.

the entire image presented here resembles very much that of a Greek philosopher.

An early ninth century icon of Nicholas with St. Zosimas, possibly painted in Palestine,[38] confronts us with a changing image (Fig. 2). His beard is now short and his hairline has receded, giving the saint a higher, more intellectual forehead. In an erect and stiff posture, Nicholas holds in his now covered left hand an elaborately decorated book. His eyes are of normal size, his gaze is directed to the left, in contrast to the earlier work where he looks straight ahead. The style of the omophorion with lobate crosses has remained the same, and the chasuble falls in soft folds. It should be noted that the definite form of his image has not yet been fully worked out in either of these works in which Nicholas appears with other saints.

One icon that might have been influential in setting the traditional St. Nicholas image is the splendid work painted in Constantinople towards the end of the tenth century[39] (Fig. 3). This is the oldest known icon of a bust of Nicholas with medallions of Christ and saints around the frame. Quite possibly, the bright colors of these medallions were inspired by the colors of cloisonné enamels. The saint's image is still naturalistic, without the symmetric lines of later works, and it is this naturalism which places the work before the eleventh century when his image was standardized in the Orthodox Church. Nevertheless, the portrait already contains all his basic characteristics: the typical lock of hair, as a new development in his iconography; the lines

---

[38] *Ibid.*, pp. 83-85.

[39] *Ibid.*, pp. 101-102.

Fig. 2. - Mount Sinai, Monastery of St. Catherine: *St. Zosimas and St. Nicholas*. Icon, early 9th century.

of the cross on his omophorion, which are now straight; and the few curved lines in his short beard. The saint gestures towards the Gospels with the long, sensitive fingers of his right hand, but the left hand remains hidden. This type of Nicholas grew to great popularity in the Orthodox Church, and his icon eventually became the fourth most important icon in the hierarchy of the iconostasis.

That Nicholas played a prominent part in the Orthodox Church is confirmed by his presence on a Deesis, dating from the eleventh century[40] and still in existence at St. Catherine. The original form of a Deesis consisted of three individual icons, located in the center of the iconostasis: a painting of the Crucifixion, flanked by an icon of the Virgin to the left and one of St. John the Baptist to the right.[41] Later, the scene of the Crucifixion found a replacement in the figure of Christ alone, and the Deesis was extended to include other religious personalities. The icon under discussion belongs to this more recent type of Deesis cycle and is painted on a single panel. Though not a product of a Constantinopolitan workshop but rather from a monastery in Syria,[42] the appearance of Nicholas on a Deesis does reveal, at an early date, a high regard for the saint. Nicholas has taken the step forward to join the two principals of Christianity, an affirmation of his role as a trusted intercessor between the worshipper and the Virgin

---

[40] SOTIRIOU, 2: 239.

[41] DAVID and TAMARA TALBOT RICE, *Icons and Their History*, New York, The Overlook Press 1974, p. 91.

[42] SOTIRIOU, 2: 239. He refers to the Nicholas Deesis: « Les icones de l'art monastique (fig. 48-53) se conforment à la tradition syriaque et leur style est plus austère ».

and Christ. As we shall see, this special relationship – particularly with the Madonna – shall not diminish over the coming centuries in the iconography of Nicholas.

While the early icons of Nicholas, such as the tenth century one from Constantinople (Fig. 3), ascribe naturalistic features to the saint, a later portrait (Fig. 4), although it contains certain similarities to the Constantinopolitan work, reflects the changes which have occurred in the meantime. This particular panel is a biographical icon, and the artist not only offers a canonical bust of Nicholas but he also avails himself of various events from the saint's life which he paints in small scenes to form a narrow band around the half-length figure of the saint. Here we shall concentrate only on the Nicholas portrait itself, as we follow the development of his canon.

The icon, painted in Sinai about the twelfth century,[43] has a more ascetic character than the earlier panels. Nicholas' features are of greater severity and geometry than in the tenth century icon, and instead of merely gesturing he now bestows a blessing with his right hand. The familiar lock of hair falls from an extremely high forehead, the hair itself has turned a dignified white. This painting from the twelfth century follows the well known canon of St. Nicholas, yet it does not seem to depart from the Constantinople

---

[43] Sotirou, 2: 244. « Au Sinai ont dû encore être executées les icones presentant des saints, en buste ou en pied, dont l'image est encadrée de petites scènes de leur vie ou de leur martyre. Les deux premières (fig. 165-166) [165 is our Fig. 4] à dater des environs du XIIe siècle, sont parmi les plus anciens speciments du genre ... ».

Kurt Weitzmann, *The Icon. Holy Images – Sixth to Fourteenth Century*, New York, G. Braziller 1978, p. 104.

icon in a radical fashion. Rather, the identifiable features of Nicholas have become frozen in strict geometric lines. At last his image has reached its definitive and unique form in the iconography of the Orthodox Church: a lock of hair on a high forehead and a short, white beard; a left hand which supports the Gospels and a right hand that blesses; and an omophorion, draped over his chasuble. These attributes of the traditional St. Nicholas, established in the eleventh century, will be continuously repeated from now on throughout the Orthodox world.

This twelfth century icon also presents us with the source for the two attributes of Gospels and omophorion. The painting refers to the legend in which Nicholas, while in jail for opposing the Arian heresy too strenuously, was presented by Christ with a copy of the Gospels and by the Virgin with an omophorion.[44] We find the figures of Christ and Mary on either side of the saint's head, one holding a book, the other a stole. This new additional iconography – the small figures of Christ and the Virgin making their presentation to Nicholas – does appear on many later St. Nicholas icons. Their divine gifts, of course, have become Nicholas' constant attributes in his canonical portrait.

Just as the image of Nicholas developed in Byzantium, so too did the scenes from his life, no doubt inspired by the wealth of literature. As already noted, his life was a subject in writings as early as the sixth century, and the legends related in manuscripts eventually also found their expression in painting. These narrative compositions were probably based on instruction books for painters, such as

---

[44] WEITZMANN, *The Icon*, p. 104.

Fig. 3. - Mount Sinai, Monastery of St. Catherine: *St. Nicholas.* Icon, 10th century.

the one in Mount Athos, which advised the artists on the structure of scenes. The book contains the description of the following ten scenes:[45]

1. Nicholas throws bags of money into a house; from the legend of the three destitute daughters;

2.-4. His ordination as deacon, priest, and bishop;

5. The awakening of a sailor on a ship; from the story of the sailor boy Ammonios;

6. The saint in prison, where he receives the Gospels and the omophorion from Christ and Mary;

7.-8. The freeing of the three innocent men at the moment of their decapitation and the appearance of Constantine and Ablabios; from the story of *The Three Stratelates*;

9. The death of the saint;

10. The Nicaean Council, where Nicholas slaps the face of Arios.[46]

---

[45] Anrich, 2: 486. « Das Malbuch vom Athos gibt Anweisung über die Komposition von Szenen aus dem Leben des Heiligen ».

[46] *Ibid.*, 2: 486. « Es sind deren neun, und zwar in der Folge des Malbuchs:

1. Nikolaus einen Geldbeutel in ein Haus werfend: Motiv aus der Geschichte von den drei Töchtern;

2.-4. Diakonen-, Priester-, Bischofsweihe;

5. Auferweckung eines Matrosen auf einem Schiff: die Geschichte vom Schiffsjungen Ammonios nach Metaphr. 9,1;

6. Der Heilige im Gefängnis, Evangelienbuch und Omophorion von Christus und Maria entgegennehmend;

7.-8. Die Befreiung der drei Unschuldigen im Augenblicke ihrer Enthauptung und die Erscheinung von Konstantin und Ablabios: zwei Motive aus der Geschichte von den Stratelaten;

9. Der Tod des Heiligen.

Dazu kommt noch die Darstellung der Nicänischen Synode, wobei Nikolaus neben Arios, im Begriffe, ihn zu ohrfeigen, im Mittelpunkt steht. Zusammen also zehn Szenen ».

Fig. 4. - Mount Sinai, Monastery of St. Catherine: *St. Nicholas.*
Central detail of biographical icon, 12th century.

According to Gustav Anrich, these compositions must have existed already before the ninth century, since the author of the Enkomion from the ninth or tenth century was moved to tears every time he looked at the scene from *The Three Stratelates.*[47]

Kurt Weitzmann argues that the narratives of the lives of saints in icon painting had their origin in the miniatures which illustrated religious manuscripts.[48] Fragments of a tiny triptych wing, harbored in St. Catherine, lend validity to this claim. Unfortunately, the wing has been cut into two sections: the top part (Fig. 5) shows the Virgin enthroned above two scenes of the ordination of St. Nicholas, one as a priest, the other as bishop; the bottom portion of the wing, not shown, depicts two narratives from the *Stratelates* as well as two scenes from the death of Nicholas. These six scenes alone have remained from a total of perhaps twenty on the original triptych.

---

[47] *Ibid.*, 2: 486. « Manche dieser Darstellungen müssen schon weit hinaufreichen. Sagt doch der im 9. oder 10. Jh. lebende Verfasser des Enkomion ..., er habe die Szene aus der Stratelatengeschichte, wie Nikolaus die drei Unschuldigen rettet, oft ... gesehen und sie nie ohne Tränen betrachten können ».

[48] Kurt Weitzmann, *Studies in Classical and Byzantine Manuscript Illumination*, Chicago, University of Chicago Press 1971, pp. 282-283. « The style of these delicately depicted scenes is so much in the tradition of the illustrated book that we must assume not only that a miniature cycle was the source, but that the icons and miniatures in instances like this actually may have been executed by the same artist ».

Sotiriou, 2: 239. Sotiriou does not believe this particular icon is stylistically miniaturist, but he agrees with Weitzmann on the date. He writes: « Dans ces deux groupes on peut encore distinguer des icones influencées par l'art monumental (fig. 42, 46, 48, 49) ... ».

Fig. 5. - Mount Sinai, Monastery of St. Catherine: *Virgin and the Ordination of St. Nicholas as Priest and Bishop.* Fragment of a triptych icon, 11th century.

This eleventh century work is the oldest example of a narrative cycle on the life of any saint in icon painting,[49] and it seems only fitting that the oldest legend, *Stratelates*, should survive on this earliest fragment containing episodes from the life of St. Nicholas. Although a triptych, its small size – the top half measures only 8 $\frac{5}{8}$ inches by 4 $\frac{3}{4}$ inches – made it just as convenient for travel as a manuscript, with the extra advantage of the durability of tempera on wood. Unlike manuscripts, however, which could only be read by an educated elite, this icon with pictorial renditions of the saint's life was sure to appeal to a wider audience, giving added impact and immediacy to the written word.

The episodes from the life of Nicholas are painted in a style not unlike the one found in the narrative painting of all other saints. Usually the legends are rendered in compositions of small figures set in simplified architectural scenes, and mere fragments of a building frequently suffice to identify the setting of a legend. In the ordination of Nicholas (Fig. 5), for instance, the architectural segments prove adequate to represent the church where this particular event from Nicholas' early life took place. Inspired by legend and instruction book, the Byzantine artist expresses the story in a condensed, straight forward manner, appropriate for the small medium of the icon and comprehensible

---

[49] WEITZMANN, *Studies in Classical and Byzantine Manuscript Illumination*, p. 282. « In the eleventh century these narrative cycles from the lives of saints invade icon painting, and the earliest example we know of is a triptych wing, now cut in two parts, which is preserved in the icon collection of Saint Catherine's Monastery on Mount Sinai. The six scenes from the life of St. Nicholas ... ».

for the worshiper. Paintings, such as the Nicholas ordination, established the pattern for later biographical icons.

All icons studied thus far were discovered in the monastery of St. Catherine and reflect purely Byzantine styles, from the capital as well as the provinces. The visual evidence suggests that Nicholas' traditional image and the illustrations of his life were well established and readily recognized in Byzantium by the end of the eleventh century. But this immediate identification was not restricted to Byzantium alone, it also applied to other countries within the Orthodox world. A brief look at a few Russian icons substantiates a continuity of Nicholas' canon and a certain adherence to Byzantine aesthetics.

Orthodox religious influence initially took root in Russian centers with the beginning of their conversion to Christianity during the tenth century. Vladimir, who ruled Kiev from 980 to 1015, brought priests, relics, sacred vessels, and icons from Constantinople,[50] and Greek artists began to open workshops in Kiev before the twelfth century. Their craft advanced even as far as Novgorod, where a Greek painter, named Petrovich in Russian, was known to be employed in 1196.[51] Novgorod's northern location deep in Russia's medieval forests had not prevented many of its citizens from traveling as pilgrims to Constantinople, Jerusalem, and Mt. Athos,[52] and the Greek artist, on his

---

[50] Timothy Ware, *The Orthodox Church*, London, Penguin Books 1963, p. 84.

[51] Gerhard, p. 144.

[52] V. N. Lazarev, *Novgorodian Icon-Painting*, trans. L. N. Feonov, Moscow, Edition « Iskusstvo » 1969, p. 12.

journey northward, probably retraced the steps of the Russian pilgrim. In addition to these religious and artistic influences, Russia also maintained secular contacts to the Byzantine Court. Mstislav Vladimirovich, a leader in Novgorod from 1096 to 1117, arranged for his daughter to marry a Greek prince, and Byzantine interest in the north was further displayed in 1186, when Novgorod was visited by the grand-nephew of the Byzantine Emperor Manuel Comnenus.[53] These timely exposures set the tone for Russian religious painting, but not without local variations from the Byzantine prototype.

When Kiev and much of central and eastern Russia fell to the Mongols in 1237-40, a large number of old icons more than likely was lost in the ensuing vandalism and destruction. Russian culture literally stagnated for the next two centuries under the yoke of the Golden Horde. Only Novgorod, which had successfully repelled the Tartarian assault and thus had remained independent, continued to flourish during the Middle Ages and became the home of a great school of icon painters. From this Novgorodian school comes one of the oldest Russian St. Nicholas icons (Fig. 6) which clearly exhibits its strong dependence on Constantinople. It was painted about the middle of the thirteenth century by a monk from the Dukhov Monastery for the Monastery of the Holy Spirit, Novgorod.[54] The panel, now in the State Russian Museum in Leningrad,

---

53 *Ibid.*, pp. 7-12.

54 *Ibid.*, pp. 13-14. YOORI A. OLSUFIEV, *The Development of Russian Icon Painting From the 12th to the 19th Century*, « Art Bulletin », 12 (Dec. 1930), 346-373.

Fig. 6. - Leningrad, State Russian Museum: *St. Nicholas.* Icon from the Monastery of the Holy Spirit, mid-13th century.

presents an austere image in a perfect Byzantine canon. Its general composition – the symmetrical facial lines, the omophorion, the blessing, the Gospels, and the intricate details of collar and cuff – offers an unmistakable replica of a Byzantine painting. No attempt at naturalism is made, every line has a symmetrical counterpart; and just as in Byzantine art, the symmetry assigns to this icon an unearthly quality of permanent stability.

Another Novgorodian icon (Fig. 7), and in appearance a particularly northern one, so it seems, also happens to be the oldest signed and dated religious painting in Russia.[55] The inscription on the lower border of the icon informs us that it was painted in 1294 by Aleksa, son of Peter, and donated by Nikolai Vasilievich.[56] This icon of Nikolai Vasilievich's patron saint was ordered for the church of St. Nicholas on the Lipna at Novgorod and now hangs in the Museum of History and Architecture, also in Novgorod. An entry in the Novgorodian Chronicle (St. Petersburg, 1879, p. 203) may support the authenticity of the work:[57]

> In the year 6801 (1294), in the reign of Prince Andrey Aleksandrovich and in that of Archbishop Clement of Novgorod and Pskov, and in that of Burgomaster Andrey Climentovich this icon of the great miracle worker Nicholas of the Lipna Monastery was painted at the order and cost of God's servant Nikolai Vasilievich in honour and glory of Nicholas the Wonder-Worker ... and in the year 7064 (1556), in the reign of the great Tsar and Grand Duke Ivan Vasilievich, Autocrat of Rus-

---

55 Talbot Rice, *Icons and Their History*, p. 99.

56 *Ibid.*, p. 99 and p. 128.

57 *Ibid.*, p. 128.

Fig. 7. - Aleksa, son of Peter: *St. Nicholas, the Miracle Worker*, Novgorod, Museum of History and Architecture. Icon from the church of St. Nicholas on the Lipna. Novgorod 1294.

sia, and in the reign of Archbishop Pimen of Novgorod the Great and Pskov, at the order and expense of Abbot Antony of Nikolsk, this image of the great miracle worker Nicholas of the Lipna Monastery was restored.

This *St. Nicholas the Miracle Worker* repeats the traditional iconography; in execution, however, it departs from the Byzantine manner. The panel displays a sharp contrast of bright colors and hard edges in the bishop's garments, the book, and the nimbus. This blaze of color creates a very decorative, Russian folk art effect that competes with and distracts from the saint's face and his small, awkward hands. Yet, the canon again remains intact amidst a local style.

Once more we see the reference to Nicholas' incarceration at the time of the Council of Nicaea in 325. On either side of the saint's head the finely painted figures of Christ and the Virgin, both standing on cushions, bestow upon Nicholas his Gospel Book and omophorion. The decoration continues along the left and right border of the icon with figures of saints while the top border contains a representation of the Deesis, symbolized by an empty throne between two Archangels who, in turn, are flanked by busts of the prophets. In this icon (Fig. 7) the artist gives us a vivid demonstration of his virtuosity in the use of color, a skill which surely must have been appreciated by his contemporaries who attended the church on the Lipna. But it is more important to recognize that Aleksa fused his considerable decorative ability with prevailing Orthodox iconography in order to create a traditionally religious, yet very Russian work of art.

Once the basic St. Nicholas image had been instituted,

it could be utilized in mediums other than the painted icon. As example may serve a Greek mosaic icon from the beginning of the fourteenth century, now in the Monastery of Stavronikita, Mount Athos [58] (Fig. 8). The mosaic cubes in this icon are of similar size as those in wall mosaic, and the technique in both cases is much alike. All components applicable to the creation of a painted Nicholas image are again evident here. Indeed, these fundamental characteristics were so well developed through the traditions of icon painting that the bishop of Myra can be identified by his head alone in the icon of *St. Nicholas* (Fig. 9), painted in Moscow in the early sixteenth century [59] and now in the possession of the Ikonenmuseum in Recklinghausen, Germany. Like all his predecessors over the centuries, the painter minimizes the natural and emphasizes the spiritual, and through the various iconographic features dedicated especially to the saint, Nicholas' portrait emerges.

The portrait, of course, was not the only subject in the Russian painter's repertoire, he also showed familiarity with the biographical icon. In the Ikonenmuseum in Recklinghausen we find that the Novgorodian school once again provides a typical example (Fig. 10); this one dates from the beginning of the sixteenth century [60] but is based on the traditional twelfth century compositions. St. Nicholas stands in the center in splendid isolation against a plain

---

[58] MANOLIS CHATZIDAKIS et al., *A Treasury of Icons From the Sinai Peninsula, Greece, Bulgaria and Yugoslavia*, p. LXXXIV.

[59] IKONEN-MUSEUM, *Kunstsammlungen der Stadt Recklinghausen*, Recklinghausen, Aurel Bongers 1968, plate 390.

[60] *Ibid.*, plate 391.

Fig. 8. - Mount Athos, Monastery of Stavronikita: *St. Nicholas*. Greek mosaic icon, beginning of 14th century.

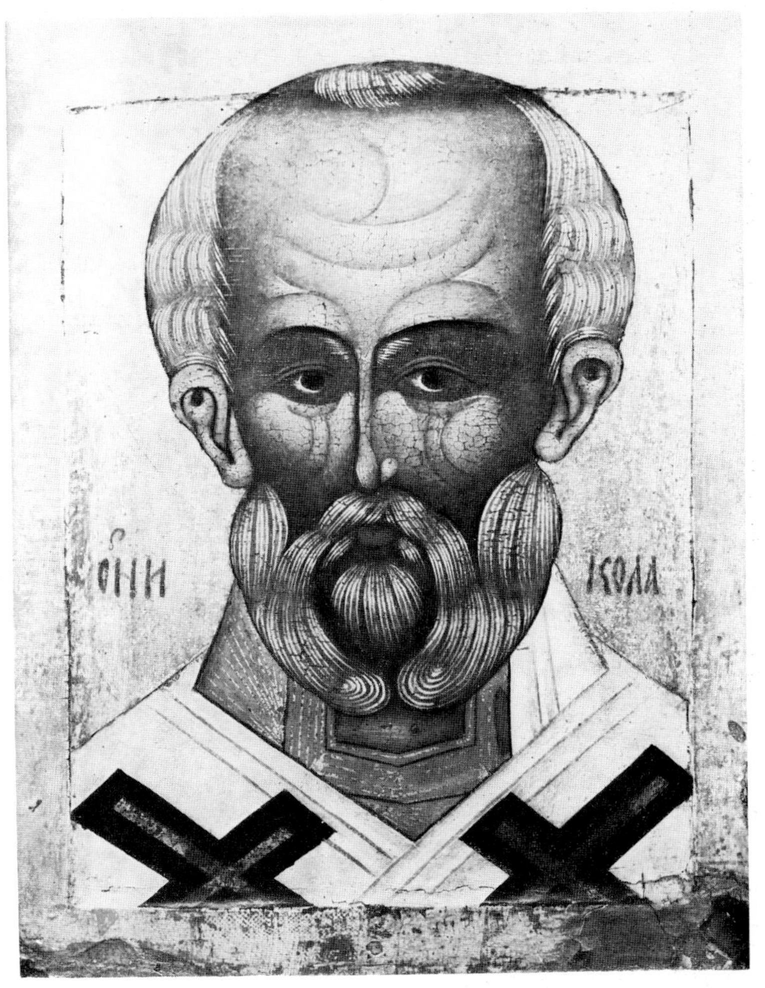

Fig. 9. - Recklinghausen, Ikonenmuseum: *St. Nicholas.* Icon from Moscow, beginning of 16th century.

background, an authoritative, patriarchal saint, surrounded by scenes from his life. The cycle presents illustrations from the birth of Nicholas to his death, and the scenes, reading left to right, are described in the Ikonenmuseum catalogue as follows:[61]

1. row: birth of St. Nicholas; baptism; instruction; ordination.

2. row: the saint appears to Emperor Constantine in his dream; he saves sailors in distress.

3. row: Nicholas rescues three innocent men from execution; he appears to the prisoners in jail.

4. row: Nicholas saves a drowning boy; he returns to the parents their son who was kidnaped by the Saracens; he is being placed in a coffin; the translation of his remains.

Not all biographical icons, however, dealt with the same stories; local tales were sometimes inserted. Nor were the legends depicted in the exact same manner. As the Russian art historian Lazarev points out, subjects from every day life and contemporary architecture were included in the

---

[61] *Ibid.*, notes to plate 391: « Um die Gestalt des hl. Nikolaus im Mittelfeld sind Szenen aus seinem Leben angeordnet. Es sind in den Reihen von links nach rechts:

1. Reihe: Geburt des hl. Nikolaus; Taufe; Unterweisung; Weihe.

2. Reihe: Der Heilige erscheint dem Kaiser Konstantin im Traum; er rettet Schiffer aus Seenot.

3. Reihe: Nikolaus rettet drei Unschuldige vor der Hinrichtung; er erscheint den Gefangenen im Kerker.

4. Reihe: Nikolaus rettet einen Ertrinkenden; er bringt den Eltern den von den Sarazenen entführten Sohn zurück; er wird in den Sarg gebettet; die Überführung seiner Gebeine ».

Fig. 10. - Recklinghausen, Ikonenmuseum: *St. Nicholas.* Biographical icon from Novgorod, beginning of 16th century.

Russian artist's design. But they never did become true genre scenes.[62]

If we analyze the biographical icons of Nicholas in general, we can determine a standard pattern: the top horizontal margin deals with his birth and ordination as priest and bishop; the two vertical frames display miracles, such as *The Three Stratelates*, *The Three Destitute Maidens*, *Saving a Ship at Sea*, and others; and the bottom horizontal concludes the cycle with the saint's death. A comparison of ordination scenes from the Byzantine triptych (Fig. 5) and the Novgorodian biographical icon (Fig. 10) proves a noticeable consistency in composition. Each individual episode in the cycle rests on the basis of a symbolic representation which clearly reduces the details of the story. The standardization of this type of icon may be a product of the notable role played by instruction books and master icons, and allows for easy recognition of scene and legend. These small compartments of bright colors, fixed around a central image, make an organized artistic whole, as all parts link together to give the icon a jewel-like setting.

A scene (Fig. 11) taken from the above mentioned early sixteenth century biographical icon fits this pattern perfectly. With a minimum of special effects, the painter has captured St. Nicholas as he saves a ship in a storm: no dramatic bolts of lightning or high, foaming waves; just a large, serene Nicholas, towering over three men who crouch apprehensively in a small boat on a dark sea. The problem of the precariously poised mariner's patron in the

---

62 Lazarev, p. 15.

Fig. 11. - Recklinghausen, Ikonenmuseum: *St. Nicholas Saves a Ship in a Storm.* Detail of Fig. 10.

bow, clad all in white, has been beautifully solved by the counterbalance of the white sail in the stern. This simple composition, characteristic of so many others, tells its story through bright colors, the merest of basic elements, and with a charm, I feel, that is unique to these diminutive segments of the biographical icon.

In review of the above Russian icons it has become obvious that, in spite of local variations, Byzantine traditions readily endured the transmigration from the sunny shores of the Aegean to the cold frontier in the north where they became the foundation for Russian religious painting. In the particular case of St. Nicholas, Russia provided fertile soil for further expansion of his cult, to which his numerous Russian icons bear witness. Retaining the spirituality of the Byzantine prototypes with great fidelity, the Russian painters proved worthy masters of their artistic inheritance.

Thanks to the protective monks of Mount Sinai, we have enough evidence today to conclude that the iconography of St. Nicholas developed slowly in Byzantium – and perhaps in conjunction with literature – until the eleventh century. The timeframe for the establishment of the saint's canon may be determined on one hand by the tenth century icon from Constantinople (Fig. 3) which seems to have been painted just before the development, and on the other hand by the twelfth century Byzantine (Fig. 4) and the thirteenth century Novgorodian (Fig. 6) icons, where his image is already fully formalized. Thus the well known characteristics of Nicholas would appear to have been finally created in the workshops of Constantinople during the eleventh century under the tutelage of the clergy. As far as the illustrations of the bishop's miracles and biographies are concerned, the fragments of the eleventh century triptych (Fig. 5) seem to indicate that the definitive cycle of those events was also formed at that time. At any rate, we recognize a repetition of patterns in similar scenes on later biographical icons. But once his canon was planted, it took root and grew into the tradition that was basically adhered to throughout the centuries and wherever icon painting was practiced in the Orthodox sphere.

Part Two

SAINT NICHOLAS IN ITALY

The Early Development of His Cult

Now that we have explored Nicholas' origin and cultivation in the East, let us follow the saint as he enters a new environment in the Catholic West. His cult blossomed next in the favorable climate of Italy, a country of geographic proximity and with close political, economic and artistic ties to Constantinople. These various affiliations may account for the very early evidence in support of the cult's presence on the Italian peninsula.

We find that the oldest reference to St. Nicholas outside Byzantium dates from 755 or 770, when his name was inscribed in the stone register of relics in the St. Angelo Church in Pescheria, Rome.[63] Also in the eighth

---

[63] Karl Meisen, *Nikolauskult und Nikolausbrauch im Abendlande. Eine kultgeographisch-volkskundliche Untersuchung*, Düsseldorf, Verlag von L. Schwann 1931, pp. 56-57.

This excellent, most detailed scholarly study is the definitive book on the Nicholas cult in Western Europe. Fortunately, it has been reissued in 1981 by Schwann-Bagel, Düsseldorf.

century, an altar dedicated to the bishop belonged to the church Santa Maria in Cosmedin in Rome, and in 792 a memorial service for him was mentioned in the Benedictine Cloister in Via lata, also in Rome.[64] Celebration of the sixth of December, his feast day, apparently occurred already at an early date and not only in Rome, for St. Nicholas' day is carved on a marble calendar, dated between 821 and 841, found in the church of St. Giovanni Maggiore in Naples.[65] In the capital, the oldest St. Nicholas church might be St. Nicola in Carcere, built alongside a prison, constructed before Pope Hadrian (772-795), near the Greek quarter of the city. Karl Meisen believes the church to date from about the same time,[66] since Nicholas was also the patron of thieves. This church had obtained a papal permission to pardon a condemned prisoner on St. Nicholas Day, an act probably suggested by the *Praxis de stratelatis*, the legend which was also the first to appear in Latin. Written before 842, it even pre-dates Nicholas' Latin biography by Johannes Diaconus of 880.[67]

---

[64] *Ibid.*, p. 58.

[65] *Ibid.*, pp. 60-61.

[66] *Ibid.*, p. 57. However, documented proof concerning the church – an inscription within the building – dates only from 1088.

[67] *Ibid.*, p. 219. « Der hervorragenden Stellung, die gerade diese Legende in der griechischen Überlieferung einnimmt, entspricht die Tatsache, dass auch in der abendländischen hagiographischen Literatur über Nikolaus diese Erzählung zuerst auftaucht und dass sie hier, jedenfalls in der älteren Zeit, für die Herübernahme des Kultes und die Entwicklung der Heiligengestalt im Abendlande eine ähnliche bedeutungsvolle Rolle gespielt hat wie in der griechischen Kirche. Im Abendlande begegnet die Legende zuerst in dem Reichenauer Codex XXXII (aus dem 9. Jahrhundert, aber vor 842), ... ».

Byzantium's and Europe's elite acted as a great moving force in the development of Nicholas' cult. We already know of the contributions by Constantine the Great, Empress Irene, and Emperor Basil I from the previous chapter, and distinguished patronage of this kind was to continue in the West, especially in southern Italy where Byzantine ideas fell upon a receptive audience. Archbishop Nicholas, who presided in Bari from 1035 to 1062 and who was the descendant of a Greek family, had two St. Nicholas churches built in Bari at his own cost.[68] Again in Bari, another St. Nicholas church was ordered by Emperor Constantine IX Monomachos (ruled 1042-1054).[69] It came to its completion during the siege of Bari by the Norman duke Robert Guiscard. After the fall of the city, the new Norman conquerors, no doubt wishing to reap the political benefits from the popularity of the holy man, wisely decided to sustain his movement. In fact, none other than St. Nicholas' image appears as the protector patron of Bari on the seal of Robert Guiscard; the seal dates from 1085.[70]

P. 527. The story of the three *Stratelates* in the Codex Augiensis XXXII, 9th century, appears in Latin pp. 527-530.

[68] *Ibid.*, p. 64. Note 3. « Zwei Urkunden des Erzbischofs Nikolaus von Bari (1035-1062) aus den Jahren 1036 und 1039 – sie wurden im Archiv der Abtei von Cava gefunden – bezeugen, dass der genannte Erzbischof, der aus einer vornehmen griechischen Familie stammte, auf seine Kosten und auf seinem Grundbesitz in oder bei Bari seinem Namenspatron zwei Kirchen errichten liess, die erste, deren zweiter Patron der hl. Basilius wurde, bei dem Orte Prandulo, die andere in Turre de Musarra ».

[69] *Ibid.*, p. 65.

[70] *Ibid.*, p. 66.

Within the realm of Byzantine influence lay also the far-reaching Benedictines whose mother monastery, Monte Cassino, was and still is located south of Rome. Throughout the eleventh century, churches and cloisters associated with the Benedictine order sprung up on behalf of the saint. Count Hugo of Tuscany, for example, established a St. Nicholas church in the Benedictine abbey in Pisa,[71] and a cloister named after the saint was built in Venice on the Lido in 1053.[72] During the same period, two Benedictine monks, Alberich and Alphanus of Salerno, set out to glorify Nicholas in a hymn.[73] Yet another connection to Byzantine art was made through Abbot Desiderius (1057-1087), who had asked Greek artists to decorate Monte Cassino.[74]

In 1087, the cult of Nicholas in Italy experienced a most important stimulus with his Translation from Myra to Bari.[75] Nicephorus, a Benedictine monk from Bari, wrote the first history of this momentous event, related to him by the merchants responsible for the Translation.[76] During the eleventh century, the Byzantine Empire had been plagued by political unrest and insecurity as a result of the

---

[71] *Ibid.*, p. 66.

[72] *Ibid.*, p. 66.

[73] *Ibid.*, p. 69, p. 253. A hymn, written by Alphanus Salerno and based on the legend of the kidnapped Basilios, reads:

> Quis non duceret hunc diem
> Festum plus reliquis, cum genitoribus
> Natos reddit ab hostibus
> Raptos ad varii servitii jugum.

[74] PAUL-HENRI MICHEL, et al., *Dictionary of Italian Painting*, London, Methuen 1964, p. 102.

[75] JACOBUS, p. 22.

[76] MEISEN, p. 94.

Turkish threat, and it was on account of this turmoil that the removal of Nicholas' remains from Myra became possible. The dispute over where the saint's new resting place should be was settled when Roger Guiscard gave the land and the permission to Archbishop Urso of Bari to construct a St. Nicholas church on the palace grounds.[77] Nicholas was laid to rest in this new church on October 1, 1089; Pope Urban II consecrated the altar and shrine in the crypt. Bari now began to flourish as a center for pilgrims, and a great hostel was erected for them by Archbishop Elias of Bari, a former Benedictine abbot.[78]

Even after the reign of the last Norman king of South Italy, royal support of Nicholas' cult was continued by Wilhelm II (1166-1189) of the German House of Hohenstaufen, and of all the St. Nicholas churches in Italy, the one in Bari was particularly favored by aristocrats, both temporal and religious. An inventory of the church in 1313 included 131 objects of gold and silver, and an additional 152 liturgical books, not including the 1296 books already in the possession of the church.[79] But the true impact of the Translation may perhaps best be measured by the great number of additional St. Nicholas churches which came into existence throughout Italy from 1087 until the end of the thirteenth century: about 74 in South Italy, approximately 56 in Rome and Central Italy, and perhaps 50 in Venice and North Italy.[80] Clearly, the cult of the saint

---

[77] *Ibid.*, p. 95.

[78] *Ibid.*, p. 98.

[79] *Ibid.*, p. 106.

[80] *Ibid.*, pp. 108-110. Meisen names all the churches and chapels on pages 108-110.

had already more than a mere foothold in Italy before the Translation; after the interment of his relics in Bari, however, Nicholas became an ever increasingly popular figure among the people and in the religion and art of Italy.

The Representation of St. Nicholas in Italian Art

Italian and Byzantine art differ vastly in concept and style, an observation which also holds true in the iconography of St. Nicholas. As concluded in our study of icons, such as the twelfth century panel in St. Catherine on Mount Sinai (Fig. 4), the image of Nicholas took on a definite, recognizable form in Byzantium during the eleventh century. In Italy, so we shall see, Nicholas' features are as varied as the styles of those who painted him. One is also immediately aware of the contrast between the Italian and Eastern manner of representing the legends. Consider as the norm the early sixteenth century *Biographical Icon of St. Nicholas* (Fig. 10), where the legends of the saint are painted in small, canonical scenes surrounding his image. Emphasis in all Byzantine and Russian art would be on religious rather than individual expression. The Italian artists, on the other hand, did not allow themselves to be constrained by a canon; instead, each of them worked in his own individual style. But before this individualism asserted itself, Byzantine painting did play a major role in the early Italian artist's work.

The oldest image of St. Nicholas in Italy dates from the eighth century and is found in Santa Maria Antiqua in Rome. The walls within this ancient church are decorated with frescoes in the Byzantine style, a not so surprising fact, as many Byzantine artists came to Rome during and after the eighth century in order to avoid the iconoclasm of the Eastern Empire.[81] Unfortunately, Santa Maria Antiqua was abandoned during the ninth century,[82] and the frescoes were neglected by the following generations, surely in part due to a lack of appreciation of the Greek painting style. One of the surviving frescoes, in damaged condition, shows a row of saints, with Christ seated in the middle. The saints of the Latin Church form a line to the right of Christ while those of the Eastern Church are positioned to His left.[83] St. Nicholas, second from the extreme right, stands rigidly among his Eastern colleagues.[84] Although the fresco has deteriorated, we can still identify Nicholas' name, written in Greek, his omophorion, and his Gospels. This work is dated by Josef Wilpert about 757-767,[85] that is

---

[81] ERNST KITZINGER, *Late Classical and Mediaeval Studies in Honor of Albert Mathias Friend, Jr. On Some Icons of the VII Century*, Princeton, Princeton University Press 1955, p. 135.

EMILE MÂLE, *The Early Churches of Rome*, trans. David Buxton, London, Ernest Benn Ltd. 1960, p. 84.

[82] MÂLE, p. 82. Note 1.

[83] *Ibid.*, p. 83.

[84] GEORGE KAFTAL, *Iconography of the Saints in Central and South Italian Schools of Painting*, Florence, Sansoni 1965, p. 800. MÂLE, p. 84 - MEISEN, pp. 25 and 29.

[85] JOSEPH WILPERT, *Die Römischen Mosaiken und Malereien der kirchlichen Bauten vom IV. bis XII. Jahrhundert*, 4 vols., Freiburg im Breisgau, Herder & C. GMBH 1924, 4: Ill. 192.. « Alttestamentlische Szenen; Christus thronend zwischen Heiligen; gemalter Teppich. Linkes Seitenschiff von Santa Maria Antiqua, von Paul I. (757-767) ».

to say, long before the canon of St. Nicholas was formed. At this point in time, Nicholas – without his name – is practically indistinguishable from other saints.

Also located in Santa Maria Antiqua is the oldest representation of a Nicholas legend, believed to be a scene from *The Three Destitute Maidens.* It was probably not painted before the ninth century, since the legend appeared first in the vita of Michael, written between 814 and 842.[86] Deterioration has made the fresco barely recognizable, but it seems to depict three young women behind a window who look with large eyes straight at the viewer. The scene is very simple, yet difficult to decipher; one might just as soon assume it to be the three *Stratelates* in prison.

The Middle Ages saw a continuation of Eastern influence in Italian art. In a thirteenth century fresco in San Lucia in Brindisi, for example, Nicholas appears so perfectly in his canon form that I believe the artist must have been Greek. As in an icon, the saint's face has beautiful geometric lines in the beard, eyes, brow, and hair; his blessing is given in the Orthodox style. Other works from the thirteenth century, although created in different media, also reflect the Byzantine dominance. To cite just a few instances: a mosaic bust of St. Nicholas at the Chapel of Santa Sanctorum in Rome; a chasuble, which illustrates several of the Nicholas legends, in Anagni; and an altarpiece in a private collection in Bisceglie. The latter contains several scenes from the life of the saint, who again bestows a Greek blessing.[87]

---

[86] MEISEN, p. 232.

[87] KAFTAL, p. 800. Kaftal's book contains several illustrations of the scenes from the altarpiece.

In the St. Nicholas church in Bari we find another source on a stone relief, dating probably from the thirteenth century, which is surrounded by episodes from his life (Fig. 12). Its design seems to be based on an Eastern model but the workmanship does not look Byzantine. The figure of the saint appears too solid and heavy for a Greek artist, and it might very well be that during the reign of the House of Anjou over the Kingdom of Naples (1266-1442) the commission for the relief was entrusted to a local sculptor. The bishop's robe is decorated with the *fleurs de lys* of the French royalty, and the second scene from the bottom, right side, illustrates the French legend – unknown in Byzantium – in which Nicholas resuscitates three students.[88] The legend holds that the saint had been traveling in his diocese and had stopped at an inn to eat. The innkeeper, who earlier had killed three journeying students, served their flesh to St. Nicholas, but the saint recognized it as such and demanded to see the bodies. This done, the saint spoke a prayer upon which the students were restored to life. As represented on the relief, the symbol of the legend is St. Nicholas standing before three small nude figures in a tub.[89] We may assume that the French rulers of South Italy were instrumental in introducing this legend to Bari.

The dominant Byzantine style in early Italian art was eventually broken by the advent of Giotto. One point that has been almost ignored by art historians was the influence

---

88 MEISEN, p. 296.

89 *Ibid.*, p. 296. This legend also appears on the back of the chasuble in Anagni.

exerted by Byzantine painting on Giotto himself. This becomes evident enough if we consider for a moment Giotto's masterpieces in the Arena Chapel in Padua where he relied upon traditional Byzantine compositions for several of the scenes.[90] In my opinion, there can be little doubt that Giotto used Byzantine prototypes as the foundation for many of his great frescoes, but within this framework he then created a more dramatic realism in painting that later artists would seek to emulate. This change of style, however, did not adversely affect the cult of Nicholas. On the contrary, the new humanism in the narrative style was particularly suited for the legends. In the remainder of this study I shall mostly consider those paintings which are related to the cycle of St. Nicholas' legends. The following works were selected as much for their artistic value as for their power of expression in rendering the stories and in revealing their important affect on Italian life.

We resume our journey, this time in search of the Italian iconography of Nicholas, in the Cappella del Sacramento in the church of San Francesco, Assisi. A fresco above the chapel's entrance introduces the donors, the two brothers Napoleone and Gian Gaetano Orsini. The younger

---

[90] To cite just some Byzantine examples which Giotto could have seen in Ravenna: *The Betrayal by Judas* in San Apollinare Nuovo and *The Baptism of Christ* in the Orthodox Baptistery and in the Arian Baptistery. Also compare the pose of Christ in *The Good Shepherd* in the lunette of the Mausoleum of Galla Placidia with the pose of the king in *The Trial by Fire* in the Bardi Chapel in Santa Croce, Florence. The design of other compositions in the Arena Chapel is even closer to Byzantine models, such as: *The Raising of Lazarus*, *Noli Me Tangere*, *Christ's Entry into Jerusalem*, and other frescoes.

ig. 12. - Bari, Church of St. Nicholas: *St. Nicholas and Scenes From His Life.* Stone relief, 13th century.

brother is dressed as a deacon, and since it is known that he became a cardinal in 1321, the frescoes in the chapel must pre-date that event.[91] While the chapel originally contained twelve scenes from the life of Nicholas, five of them are now almost obliterated. The surviving scenes come from the legends of *The Three Stratelates* (three frescoes), *Adeodatus* (two frescoes), *The Jew Who Owned a St. Nicholas Icon*, and *The Three Destitute Maidens* (one fresco each). Those which are almost destroyed include: *St. Nicholas Saving a Ship in a Storm*; *The Miracle of the Corn Ships*; and *Nicholas Restoring a Maiden to Life*.[92] The artist of these paintings is unknown, but more than likely he was a follower of Giotto, for he adheres closely to the style of the great Florentine master.

The scenes from *The Three Stratelates* read as follows: St. Nicholas as he saves three men from the executioner (Fig. 13); as he forgives the guilty consul who ordered the execution of the three men (Fig. 14); and as he appears to Constantine while he sleeps (Fig. 15). We notice a remarkable difference in style here in comparison to the thirteenth century paintings. A much higher degree of naturalism is present in the later works; the architecture is more detailed, the figures more realistic, and the artist's attempt to tell the story through dramatic presentation proves highly successful. Quite the same is true in the frescoes which depict the *Adeodatus* legend.[93] The boy

---

[91] OSWALD SIRÉN, *Giotto and Some of His Followers*, 2 vols., Cambridge, Harvard University Press 1917, 2: 97.

[92] *Ibid.*, 2: 97-98.

[93] JACOBUS, p. 24. - MEISEN, p. 253.

Fig. 13. - Assisi, Cappella del Sacramento in the Church of San Francesco: *St. Nicholas Saves Three Men From Execution*. Fresco.

Fig. 14. - Assisi, Cappella del Sacramento in the Church of San Francesco
St. Nicholas Forgives the Guilty Consul. Fresco.

Fig. 15. - Assisi, Cappella del Sacramento in the Church of San Francesco: *St. Nicholas Appears in Constantine's Dream.* Fresco.

Adeodatus was kidnapped and taken to a foreign country but is returned to his parents the following year on St. Nicholas' day by the saint himself. The fresco deals with the legend in two scenes (Fig. 16). In the top segment the saint swoops down to snatch Adeodatus from slavery, and in the bottom composition Nicholas presents the lost son to his surprised family. For best dramatic effect the painter selected the two moments in which the saint himself is involved in the story.

Four panels, also taking their theme from Nicholas legends, are among the best work of Ambrogio Lorenzetti, one of Siena's greatest painters. It is not known when Lorenzetti was born, only that he died during the plague in 1348. The panels may be from Ambrogio's middle period [94] and were painted for an altarpiece for San Procolo in Florence.[95] The represented legends are: *The Three Destitute Maidens* (Fig. 17), *The Consecration of St. Nicholas* (Fig. 18), *The Revival of a Possessed Child* (Fig. 19), and *The Miracle of the Corn Ships* (Fig. 20). As one of the more popular legends in Italy the story of the three maidens was readily identified with St. Nicholas and it became a beloved subject among artists. The legend speaks of a poor nobleman with three daughters who were unable to marry because they had no dowry. Nicholas, while still

---

94 George Rowley, *Late Classical and Mediaeval Studies in Honor of Albert Mathias Friend, Jr. The S. Niccolò Narratives by Ambrogio Lorenzetti*, Princeton, Princeton University Press 1955, p. 390.

95 Sir J. A. Crowe and G. B. Cavalcaselle, ed. by Edward Hutton, *A New History of Painting in Italy*, 3 vols., London, Dent 1908-09, 2: 92.

Fig. 16. - Assisi, Cappella del Sacramento in the Church of San Francesco: *St. Nicholas Saves Adeodatus From Slavery and Returns Him to His Parents.* Fresco.

Fig. 17. - Ambrogio Lorenzetti: *The Three Destitute Maidens*, Florence, Uffizi. Wing of triptych, c. 1327-32.

Fig. 18. - Ambrogio Lorenzetti: *Consecration of St. Nicholas*, Florence, Uffizi. Wing of triptych, c. 1327-32.

a young man and before he had been appointed to the office of bishop, heard of their dilemma and decided to solve their problem by secretly giving each of them a bag

Fig. 19. - AMBROGIO LORENZETTI: *St. Nicholas Revives a Child Strangled by the Devil*, Florence, Uffizi. Wing of triptych, c. 1327-32.

of gold. He threw the dowry into their house on three consecutive nights and thus saved the young women from a life of prostitution.[96] The three bags of gold were

---

96 ANRICH, 2: 261. - JACOBUS, p. 17. - MEISEN, p. 232.

transformed by Italian artists into three golden spheres which consequently became a favorite symbol of St. Nicholas in Italian art. Ambrogio tells the tale in one scene by dividing the composition into exterior and interior areas.

Fig. 20. - AMBROGIO LORENZETTI: *The Miracle of the Corn Ships*, Florence, Uffizi. Wing of triptych, c. 1327-32.

Unseen by the beneficiaries, the saintly man has just thrown the gold in form of spheres to the desolate and surprised family inside the house, but through the device of open architecture Lorenzetti permits the viewer to observe the story from both sides.

Ambrogio again takes advantage of an architectural scheme in the consecration panel when he accommodates two episodes within a singular space. The young Nicholas has just entered the church in the foreground and is about to be selected as the new bishop of Myra because he was the first to step into the church that day, thereby fulfilling a prophesy which had predicted this event.[97] The second scene portrays the consecration of Nicholas who kneels before the altar. Both scenes are designed in such a fashion that they appear to be one, united in the realistic space and architecture of the chapel.

The painting of *The Revival of a Possessed Child* is Ambrogio's most complicated narrative. It recreates one of the saint's posthumous miracles and tells of a young boy who was strangled by the devil while his family celebrated St. Nicholas Day. After the father begged Nicholas for help, the boy was restored to life.[98] Lorenzetti, taking us on a short trip through the narrative, begins in the upstairs room where the family commemorates the saint's day of honor. The next step brings us to the top of the stairway where the little boy stands facing the devil. We continue on down the staircase to discover the boy's strangulation. The last scene again presents an exterior and interior relationship. With the dead boy and his distraught family in the lower bedroom hope is nearby, for our saint floats above the devil on the stairs from where he beams his life-giving rays through the window to the boy on the bed. Ambrogio managed to render the narrative exquisitely by

---

[97] JACOBUS, p. 18.

[98] JACOBUS, p. 23. - MEISEN, p. 284.

dividing his space into units, then combining them again through the architectural setting. The link between architecture and participants of the drama is quite well accomplished in what is probably the most eloquent episode in narrative painting.

Finally, the fourth legend on Ambrogio's panel is *The Miracle of the Corn Ships.* Meisen gives three versions of this miracle, but they all acknowledge that St. Nicholas saved his diocese from famine.[99] In order to relieve his people from starvation, Nicholas convinced the captains of some grain ships to deliver corn to Myra after he had assured them that they would find the corn to weigh the same as before upon arrival at their destination, thus fulfilling the required quota.[100] Ambrogio meets the demands of the story by setting it in a deep seascape rather than in a small harbor.[101] Nicholas stands at shore and has persuaded the captains to unload the corn. The seamen are already in the process of emptying the ships while angels overhead replenish the cargo by pouring fresh golden corn into the boats. Lorenzetti's bright colors in all the scenes constitute a remnant of the Byzantine effect on Sienese painting, making these small panels truly gems of Italian art.

The Cappella Castellani in the church of Santa Croce, Florence, possesses frescoes of the following St. Nicholas legends: *The Jew and the Cheating Christian* (Fig. 21);

---

[99] MEISEN, p. 250.

[100] ANRICH, 2: 261. - JACOBUS, p. 19. - MEISEN, p. 250.

[101] ROWLEY, p. 390. « ... the first convincing western seascape ».

Fig. 21. - Florence, Cappella Castellani in the Church of Santa Croce: *The Jew and the Cheating Christian.* Fresco.

St. Nicholas Rescues the Drowned Boy (Fig. 22); *St. Nicholas as He Stops an Execution*, taken from *The Three Stratelates* (Fig. 23); and *The Three Destitute Maidens* (Fig. 24). At one time these works were attributed to Agnolo Gaddi, but now they are believed to be by one of his followers; no one, however, can determine the artist with certainty. The frescoes were part of a commission, disclosed in a will of 1383 which states that Ser Michele di Vanni Castellani left 1,000 florins for the erection and decoration of a burial chapel for himself and his heirs.[102] As Castellani had been a wealthy banker,[103] the legend of *The Jew and the Cheating Christian* (Fig. 21) is particularly relevant because it associates Nicholas with the profession of moneylenders.

The narrative begins on the right side of the fresco when a Christian borrows some gold from a Jew. The Christian vows before a St. Nicholas altar to return the money on a certain day. When that day comes, he refuses to pay his debt and the case goes to court. The debtor brings with him a hollow cane, filled with the borrowed gold. The middle section of the fresco shows the Jew holding the cane while the Christian swears that he has returned all he owes, and the case is dismissed. It so happens that the Christian on his way home from court falls asleep by the roadside and is killed by a runaway cart. This impact also breaks the stick, spilling the gold onto the street for all to see. The final scene on the left reveals

---

102 BRUCE COLE, *Agnolo Gaddi*, Oxford, Oxford University Press 1977, p. 78.

103 COLE, p. 79.

Fig. 22. - Florence, Cappella Castellani in the Church of Santa Croce: *St. Nicholas Rescues a Drowned Boy.* Fresco.

the Christian pinned under the wheels of the cart, the broken cane by his side, while the Jew kneels next to the wagon. The legend concludes with the refusal of the Jew to take his money unless St. Nicholas restores the Christian to life. The saint complies with this wish and the Jew converts to Christianity. Although the fresco does not actually show the closing part, it is implied by the pleading gesture of the Jew, his head raised towards Nicholas in the sky above.[104] The artist has clearly recounted the story, but he was unable to integrate three such disparate scenes into one cohesive entity.

Since the name of St. Nicholas was employed by Italian bankers as they took an oath, this legend might have been ordered by the banker Castellani to remind debtors of their obligations. In addition, Italy's most famous banking family, the Medici, used the saint's symbol of the three golden spheres on their coat of arms.[105] We also find the same symbol displayed by pawnbrokers, which points perhaps to another derivative of the legend.

As already mentioned, the three golden spheres became a common attribute of the saint in Italian art. One very early example possibly shows us the source for this simplified symbolism taken from *The Three Destitute Maidens* legend. The scene (Fig. 25) is an illumination from Ludwig Ms. VI 6 fol. 171*v* in the J. Paul Getty Museum in Malibu, California. The miniature in this antiphony was created in

---

[104] JACOBUS, p. 22 - MEISEN, p. 281.
[105] MEISEN, p. 284.

Fig. 23. - Florence, Cappella Castellani in the Church of Santa Croce: *St. Nicholas Stops an Execution*, from *The Three Stratelates*. Fresco.

Fig. 24. - Florence, Cappella Castellani in the Church of Santa Croce: *The Three Destitute Maidens.* Fresco.

Fig. 25. - Malibu, J. Paul Getty Museum: *St. Nicholas and the Three Maidens.* Ludwig Ms. VI 6 fol. 171*v*, detail, circa end of 13th century.

Florence about the end of the thirteenth century,[106] and it is believed that the manuscript itself originated in a Dominican Scriptorium.[107] A most unusual feature of the composition presents a problem in that the illuminator depicts only two maidens and two bags of gold. Whither the artist intended to paint two of each to indicate the saint's visit on the second night or whether he did so out of ignorance or simply for aesthetic reasons is not clear. What we can state, however, is that the composition reveals its early Italian influence and that it was probably painted by a miniaturist in the workshop of Cimabue.[108] But it is really the figure of St. Nicholas which holds our particular interest here as he carries the golden spheres and turns towards the singer of the hymn. This type of Nicholas would appear to be the prototype for later figures, easily identified as the Bishop of Myra by his special attribute, the legendary gift to the three young women.

Of the numerous available examples of this iconography I chose for illustration a wing panel from an altarpiece by Agnolo Gaddi, dated c 1395, now in the Alte Pinakothek in Munich (Fig. 26). Because of its enormous size, Bruce Cole thinks that this altarpiece could have been « the most monumental of the entire Trecento in Florence ».[109] In Agnolo's panel, Nicholas supports the golden spheres with

---

106 ANTON VON EUW und JOACHIM M. PLOTZEK, *Die Handschriften der Sammlung Ludwig*, Köln, Schnütgen-Museum 1979, 1: 285-286.

107 *Ibid.*, 1: 285.

108 *Ibid.*, 1: 286.

109 COLE, p. 42. The predella and wing measure almost 2 ¼ meters.

Fig. 26. - AGNOLO GADDI: *St. Nicholas*, Munich, Alte Pinakothek. Wing from an altarpiece, c. 1395.

his left hand, yet this is not a consistent element in the iconography; other painters choose to place them in his right hand. In addition to the wing panel, the Alte Pinakothek also owns two predella panels from the same altarpiece, *St. Nicholas and the Three Destitute Maidens* (Fig. 27) and *St. Nicholas As He Saves a Ship in a Storm* (Fig. 28). When we look at Nicholas, we are treated to a contrasting study in formality: the saint as the frontal, stately bishop on the wing panel and then as a profiled, casual young man in *The Three Maidens.* On account of their similarity, these panels are said to be by the same artist who painted the St. Nicholas scenes in the Castellani Chapel,[110] but I personally feel that the frescoes are the better works of art. The frescoes, Figs. 22 and 24, convey a more harmonious relationship between the figures and the space they occupy, whereas the rather monumental figures in the two predella panels seem too large for their tight, enclosed surroundings. Any feeling for space, movement and narrative remains muted.

A painting that overcomes all the failings of the previous panels is the Quaratesi altarpiece by Gentile di Niccolò di Giovanni di Maso, known as Gentile da Fabriano. Vasari said of this masterpiece:

> In the church of San Niccolò, situated at the gate of Miniato, Gentile da Fabriano painted the picture for the high altar, a work which appears to me much superior to any other that I have seen from his hand. For to say nothing of the Virgin surrounded by numerous Saints, which are all extremely well

110 *Ibid.*, p. 43.

Fig. 27. - Agnolo Gaddi: *The Three Destitute Maidens,* Munich, Alte Pinakothek. Predella, c. 1395.

Fig. 28. - Agnolo Gaddi: *St. Nicholas Saves a Ship in a Storm*, Munich, Alte Pinakothek. Predela, c. 1395.

done, the predella of this picture, covered with stories from the life of San Niccolò, in small figures, could not possibly be more beautiful nor more perfectly executed than it is.[111]

The altarpiece was commissioned in 1425 by Bernardino di Castello Quaratesi, a man who held many important public offices in Florence, such as Prior in 1376, 1392, 1404, and 1408, and Chief Magistrate of the Republic in 1419.[112] Unfortunately, today the altarpiece is divided among four museums in three different countries. The center panel is in the Royal Collection, London, the four wing panels in the Uffizi, Florence; four predella panels in the Vatican Gallery, Rome; and one panel in the National Gallery, Washington.

If all those scattered panels were reassembled, they would not only allow us to behold a superb and impressive altarpiece, but they would at the same time instill in us a deeper appreciation of the significant relationship between St. Nicholas and the Virgin, alike the one we have already encountered in Byzantine painting. The reconstruction would assign to the Nicholas wing panel the place of honor on the Virgin's immediate right, an ideal position from which he could act as an intermediary between the worshipper and the Madonna. For that role he wears a sumptuous robe and miter, this time holding the three golden spheres

---

[111] Giorgio Vasari, *Lives of Seventy of the Most Eminent Painters, Sculptors and Architects*, edited and annotated by E. H. and E. W. Blashfield and A. A. Hopkins, New York, Scribner's Sons 1911, 2 vols., 2: 97.

[112] Lionel Cust and Herbert Horn, *Quaratesi Altarpiece*, « Burlington Magazine », VI, 1905, 470-473, p. 473.

Fig. 29. - GENTILE DA FABRIANO: *St. Nicholas' Birth*, Rome, Vatican Pinacoteca. Predella from the Quaratesi altarpiece, 1427.

in his right hand. In the painting of the important wing panel, Gentile decided to represent an aloof Nicholas in the rich, courtly International Style, but for the smaller, less eye-catching predella panels he portrays the other side of the saint, a Nicholas closer to the common people.

The first of the Vatican pictures focuses on a scene from Nicholas' birth (Fig. 29), namely, the moment when the saint stood up in his bath on the day he was born.[113] While the child stands before an open fire, his mother remains in bed in the inner room. With the scene set in a contemporary interior, this panel conveys a warm, domestic atmosphere. In the second painting, which again takes its theme from the legend of the three maidens (Fig. 30), Nicholas has climbed to reach a high window outside the house, where we find him engaged in the act of throwing the third bag of gold into the room. The red bedcover, on which the first two golden bags rest, enhances the illusion of depth within a simple chamber. According to the *Golden Legend*, this event takes place at night, and Gentile accurately has the family prepare for bed in what looks like an every day routine, only to be interrupted by their patron's generosity.

The next Vatican predella panel turns from the genre to the dramatic: *St. Nicholas Saving a Ship at Sea* (Fig. 31). A fierce wind has almost torn the ship's sails asunder, and the crew hastens to lighten the boat by throwing cargo overboard. Rescue is imminent, however, as the protector of seamen flies toward the distressed ship in a cloud of golden light. Gentile recaptures vividly the dangers of the

---

[113] JACOBUS, p. 68.

Fig. 30. - GENTILE DA FABRIANO: *The Three Destitute Maidens*, Rome, Vatican Pinacoteca. Predella from the Quaratesi altarpiece, 1427.

Fig. 31. - Gentile da Fabriano: *St. Nicholas Saves a Ship in a Storm*, Rome, Vatican Pinacoteca. Predella from the Quaratesi altarpiece, 1427.

stormy sea, where strange creatures swim under the surface. Indeed, protection by the patron of mariners is a necessity in this hazardous situation.

Of all the Vatican panels, the most uncommon is the representation of *St. Nicholas As He Resuscitates Three Students* (Fig. 32). This legend, as it appears on a stone relief in Bari, has been discussed earlier, and I had pointed out that it probably sprung from French origin. Now the legend emerges on the Quaratesi altarpiece, and we may wonder where or how Gentile came across this episode from the saint's life. This is the only narrative from the Quaratesi predella panels which cannot be discovered in the *Golden Legend.* Gentile da Fabriano was, of course, a consummate artist who, like a medieval journeyman, traveled throughout Italy to complete his commissions, and it must have been on his travels that he learned of this legend. If Vasari is correct, Gentile did in fact visit Bari, where he might even have seen the stone relief already referred to above. Vasari reports:

> ... and a Crucifix, which, after having painted, he cut from the wood, in Sant'Agostino in Bari; with three very beautiful figures in half-length, which are over the entrance to the choir.[114]

Gentile's painting of the legend is wonderfully detailed. Nicholas, dressed in his bishop's regalia, stands before three young and nude men in tubs. Behind the bishop, the innkeeper and his wife kneel and beg forgiveness for their

---

[114] VASARI, 2: 97.

Fig. 32. - GENTILE DA FABRIANO: *St. Nicholas Resuscitates Three Scholars*, Rome, Vatican Pinacoteca. Predella from the Quaratesi altarpiece, 1427.

terrible deed. In front of the open door, a man sits at a table and drinks, indicating that the establishment is an inn.

The final panel, now in the National Gallery, Washington, presents *The Miracle of St. Nicholas' Tomb* (Fig. 33). Ambrogio Lorenzetti's church in his painting of *The Consecration of St. Nicholas* (Fig. 18) apparently has influenced Gentile's design of columns, curving ceiling beams, side aisles, and steps. Naturally, the details are as different as the stories. The miracle in Gentile's work is unmistakable: a cured man walks away from the tomb, his crutches over his shoulder, while others, still hoping for a miracle, are carried or hobble on crutches toward the tomb.[115] Behind the sarcophagus, segments of five scenes from St. Nicholas' life are believed by Wilhelm Suida to be identical with those of the predella from the Quaratesi altarpiece.[116] In this panel, as in the others, Gentile has proved himself a masterful storyteller with a richness in narrative details, his scenes set in realistic space and described in bright colors.

An even more impressive work of art, the altarpiece in the Galleria Nazionale dell'Umbria (Fig. 34), comes to us from the hand of the saintly Fra Angelico. This polytych was initially painted for the chapel of San Niccolò dei Guidalotti in San Domenico, Perugia. Commissioned in the will of Bishop Benedetto Guidalotti, who died in 1429, the painting was not finished until 1437.[117] One of the

---

115 JACOBUS, p. 21.

116 WILHELM SUIDA, *Two Unpublished Paintings by Gentile da Fabriano*, « Art Quarterly », 3, 1940, 348-352, p. 351.

117 JOHN POPE-HENNESSY, *Fra Angelico*, New York, Cornell University Press 1974, p. 5.

Fig. 33. - Gentile da Fabriano: *The Miracle of St. Nicholas' Tomb*, Washington, National Gallery. Predella from the Quaratesi altarpiece, 1427.

Fig. 34. - FRA ANGELICO: *Virgin and Child Enthroned with Four Angels between Saints Dominic, Nicholas, John the Baptist, and Catherine of Alexandria*, Perugia, Galleria Nazionale dell'Um-

wing panels features Nicholas in full figure, and on the predella Fra Angelico gives new life to the by now familiar Nicholas legends. We can easily imagine how the holy friar would enjoy this particular and appropriate subject, for an early document specifically associates the artist with the cult of Nicholas. In it, the miniaturist Battista di Biagio Sanguigni proposes Fra Angelico on October 31, 1417, for membership of the Compagnia di San Niccolò in the church of the Carmine in Florence.[118] It proved the fate of the painting to be taken by the French during the Napoleonic wars from Perugia to Paris, only to be returned after the French had lost the war. Two predella panels, however, went to the Vatican.

Fra Angelico has created an extraordinary St. Nicholas in this work. The bishop of Myra again stands in the place of honor to the right of the Virgin and is shown without his miter which sits on a table, almost hidden from view. Inspite of his luxurious golden vestments, Nicholas' magnificent bald head emenates a strong ascetic and studious character. It is apparent that the artist has imparted his own intense religious feelings into this panel.

One of the Vatican panels describes three scenes from the early life of Nicholas (Fig. 35). The story begins on the left, where he stands up in his bath on the day of his birth, his mother still confined to bed. This idea corresponds to Gentile's treatment of the same legend. In the center scene, the young Nicholas listens to a sermon, obviously before he was selected as bishop of Myra. The story of *The Three Maidens* takes place in the house on the right.

---

118 *Ibid.*, p. 198.

Fig. 35. - Fra Angelico: *St. Nicholas' Birth. St. Nicholas Listens to a Sermon. The Three Destitute Maidens*, Rome, Vatican Pinacoteca. Predella from the Perugia altarpiece, 1437.

It is the achievement of Fra Angelico that he managed to unite three separate episodes of the saint's life into one harmonious, architecturally balanced street scene.

The other painting at the Vatican also couples variant legends, but this time the demand is for a different environment, the sea (Fig. 36). On the left side, *The Miracle of the Corn Ships* is depicted in bright, clear daylight. The legend of *The Ship in a Storm*, on the other hand, occurs under a darkened sky on a threatening ocean. As in Gentile's painting of the same subject, a strange sea monster lurks close by, perhaps in anticipation of a shipwreck. The last predella panel of the altarpiece hangs in Perugia, Galleria Nazionale dell'Umbria. In contrast to the other compositions, Fra Angelico makes no attempt to unite the two scenes which pay tribute to *St. Nicholas' Rescue of Three Men from Execution*, from the legend of the *Stratelates*, and to *The Death of St. Nicholas* (Fig. 37). Rather, the artist consciously divides these episodes through a center wall. Nevertheless, though not linked in a physical sense, the legends enjoy a common spirit; for just as the condemned men find salvation, so too does St. Nicholas when he is received by the angels above his death bed. This monumental altarpiece is an outstanding example of Fra Angelico's thoughtful narrative, his exhibit of excellent colors, fine treatment of space, and deep religious feeling.

A fitting climax to our tour of Italian iconography is provided by a painting from the Renaissance which, in a sense, sums up the esteemed role of St. Nicholas in Italian art. The *Madonna in Glory with Six Saints* (Fig. 38) was painted by Titian about 1535 for the church of San Niccolò dei Frari in Venice. In 1770 the altarpiece was cut

Fig. 36. - FRA ANGELICO: *The Miracle of the Grain Ships. St. Nicholas Saves a Ship in a Storm*, Rome, Vatican Pinacoteca. Predella from the Perugia altarpiece, 1437.

Fig. 37. - Fra Angelico: *St. Nicholas Stops an Execution. The Death of St. Nicholas*, Perugia, Galleria Nazionale dell'Umbria. Predella from the Perugia altarpiece, 1437.

in half in order to transport it to Rome, where it was reassembled and then bought by Clement XIV. Shortly after that, the original top semicircular section was removed to make the painting rectangular and thus compatible to be placed next to Raphael's *Transfiguration.*[119]

Titian probably cannot be credited with painting the entire altarpiece, but the hand of the master certainly executed the upper half of Nicholas, the figure of St. Catherine, and the head of St. Peter.[120] Although the rest of the panel is said to be painted by Titian's brother Francesco,[121] the Venetian master most assuredly conceived the composition, a design of particular interest to us because of its special iconography.

The physical isolation of the Virgin and Child above from the saints below would be strange enough even if the Dove of the Holy Spirit, which remained on the removed top section, had been kept as an integral part of the painting. Instead of distributing equal eminence to each figure in this *sacra conversazione*, Titian chose to assemble the six saints, Catherine of Alexandria, Nicholas, Peter, Francis of Assisi, Anthony of Padua, and Sebastian, in a loose group. Titian's intent, it seems to me, was to leave the bishop of Myra as the sole link between the Madonna and Child on their remote island in heaven and those who approach with reference the altar in the church. The other saints,

---

119 WILLIAM HOOD and CHARLES HOPE, *Titian's Vatican Altarpiece and the Pictures Underneath*, « Art Bulletin », LIX, 1977, 534-552. See this article for a thorough discussion of the date and painting.

120 *Ibid.*, p. 543.

121 *Ibid.*, p. 543 Also note 39.

Fig. 38. - TITIAN: *Madonna in Glory with Six Saints*, Rome, Vatican Pinacoteca. Oil painting, c. 1535.

painted mostly in subdued colors and relegated to minor positions, pay scant attention to Virgin or congregation: St. Catherine, a slim profile on the left, looks down; an almost hidden and preoccupied St. Peter reads the bishop's gospels; St. Francis and St. Anthony turn away from the viewer and almost blend into the background; and St. Sebastian, finally, appears altogether removed in thought and presence from his saintly companions. Nicholas, on the other hand, stands boldly in the foreground, his head raised in direction of the Virgin. Prominent in placement and sheer bulk, attired in glowing vestments, he clearly emerges as *primus inter pares.* Attracted at first by color and weight, the worshipper's eye is guided along the golden ceremonial robe towards Nicholas' uplifted, spiritual head. I find this beautifully painted head to be the pivot of Titian's iconography, for it is from here that the saint's transcendental gaze presents the only direct line of communication from those on earth to the Virgin in Glory. At the same time, it is possible to interpret Nicholas' massive figure as a bridge over which the congregation gains access to the still visible rays, symbolic of God's love, that had descended from the Dove of the Holy Spirit.

Titian's altarpiece for San Niccolò dei Frari was typical of many other commissions in St. Nicholas' honor. A thousand years and more after his death, Nicholas inspired rich and powerful men to dedicate chapels, churches, frescoes, and altarpieces in his name. Yet numbers alone do not sufficiently explain the true force the saint exerted on Italian life. The penetration of his spiritual influence, I believe, is best expressed in the splendid altarpieces; of these, such exquisitely painted legends as those by Ambrogio

Lorenzetti, Gentile da Fabriano, and Fra Angelico held a special value. It was the accomplishment of the Italian artist, with his wonderful narrative expressions, to present visual images which could be immediately comprehended by the general audience. This, in turn, aided the development of the St. Nicholas cult among the broader populace which could relate to the eloquence of these picture stories. The thirteenth century Byzantine influence on Italian art had been strong, and some of the motifs lingered on until much later periods. But the Italian artist would bring the aloof spiritualism of Byzantine art down to earth and, as a consequence, St. Nicholas to a more human plane.

Part Three

SAINT NICHOLAS IN NORTHERN EUROPE

His Cult Emerges North of the Alps

The two previous chapters dealt with the origin, establishment, and acceptance of Nicholas' cult in Byzantium, the East, and the Italian peninsula. But could the movement, which had so effortlessly traversed the vast Steppes of Russia, also surmount the formidable barrier of the mighty Alps and conquer the North? Indeed, the cult found easier access to northern Europe than one would imagine, basically through three diverse heralds: the aristocrat, the sailor, and the pilgrim. The Alpine chain, of course, posed no obstacle to the Norman mariner who sailed from the ports of southern Italy and Byzantium to those of northern Europe. There he could relate the wondrous deeds of his patron saint which he had discovered on his foreign travels. Yet word about Nicholas was also carried northward on land, along the Po valley and over the mountains, by the many pilgrims returning from the holy places of Italy and Palestine. These messengers by land and sea contributed in no small measure to the introduction and later popularization of the cult in northern Europe. Finally, as it was the case in all the countries discussed so far, the aristocracy again proved a standard-bearer for Nicholas, this time in the establishment of the cult north of the Alps. A strong impulse came directly from the Byzantine court in the person of princess Theophano.

For the earliest documentary evidence on Nicholas in France and Germany, we must look to the holy literature of the ninth century, where we find, among other references to his name, an account of the legend of the three *Stratelates*.[122] By the late tenth century, his feast day was known well enough to be recorded in the church calendars of western Europe.[123] This period of the tenth century also saw the beginning of an active phase of dedications to Nicholas, generally churches, abbeys or monasteries, which were primarily sponsored at this stage by the German kings and Holy Roman emperors of the Ottonian House. The pronounced royal interest in Nicholas coincided with the marriage of Otto II (955-83) to the Byzantine princess Theophano in 972, an occasion which obviously intensified the cultural relationship between the German court and Byzantium. The mere fact of the marriage proves that the Ottonians already maintained connections with the East and thus might have possibly come into contact with the Nicholas cult before 972. But the flurry of dedications to Nicholas after the wedding leads us to conclude that the

---

122 MEISEN, pp. 73-74.
123 *Ibid.*, p. 81.

eastern saint, so popular in Byzantium, had now also become a favorite patron among the aristocrats in the North.

Just one year after Princess Theophano's arrival at the Ottonian court, a St. Nicholas chapel was consecrated in the cloister Kempten im Allgäu in southern Germany.[124] Bishop Udalrich of Augsburg, who performed the consecration, had received the cloister from Theophano's father-in-law, Otto the Great (912-73). In 987, Archbishop Willigis of Mainz (975-1011), the teacher of Otto II, dedicated a church to Nicholas in Weende, near Göttingen, in northern Germany.[125] Yet Theophano's influence was also witnessed within the immediate royal family. Her son, Otto III (980-1002), erected the cloister Burtscheid, located in the vicinity of Aachen, placing it under the patronage of Nicholas and appointing a Byzantine monk, Gregor, as the cloister's abbot.[126] Later, the same Gregor would build a St. Nicholas chapel on the site of an old St. Peter church,

---

124 *Ibid.*, p. 80.

125 *Ibid.*, p. 82.

126 *Ibid.*, p. 82. « Dem mittelbaren Einflusse der Kaiserin Theophano wird man dann aber die Wahl des hl. Nikolaus als Patron des Klosters Burtscheid bei Aachen zuschreiben dürfen, das von Otto III. vor 1000 errichtet wurde. In den *Brunwilarensis monasterii fundatorum acta 10* wird als Grund für die Wahl des hl. Nikolaus als Patron ausdrücklich angeführt, dass auch Otto von mütterlicher Seite ein Grieche gewesen sei ... Ein byzantinischer Mönch Gregor, der nach Zerstörung seines heimatlichen Klosters nach Italien in ein Benediktinerkloster gekommen war und vom Kaiser die Abtstelle in Burtscheid erhielt, soll an der Stelle einer alten Peterskirche zwei neue Kapellen, eine zu Ehren des hl. Apollinaris, die andere zu Ehren des hl. Nikolaus, errichtet haben. Mit den Namen dieser beiden Heiligen wird das Kloster in einer Urkunde von 1016 genannt. In die Nikolauskapelle soll durch Gregor auch ein Bild des hl. Nikolaus aus dem Orient gekommen sein, ... ».

for which he commissioned – probably from Constantinople – a mosaic icon (Fig. 39). The saint does bestow a Latin blessing in this representation, but style and workmanship of the icon clearly point to Byzantium.

Again in Aachen, the royal house endowed a religious school, where students had the opportunity to worship in a St. Nicholas chapel. A document of Heinrich II, dated 1005, refers to the school as well as to a « *festivitas sancti Nicholai* ».[127] Today, perhaps as a testimony to the cult's continuity, a St. Nicholas parish church still occupies the same spot. And if any further proof was required about Theophano's lasting effect on her offsprings, it was provided by Count Ezzo of the Palatine, who, in 1024 and in honor of the bishop of Myra, built the Benedictine abbey Brauweiler, near Cologne. Count Ezzo was none other than the husband of Mathilde, Theophano's daughter.[128]

In the eleventh century, church and abbey construction also flourished in France, and our saint was not neglected in the consecration of these holy institutions. Foundation of the abbey St. Nicolas in Angers, for example, took place in 1020, and in 1022 the church St. Nicolas-les-Arras was built in Artois.[129] The early arrival of the cult in France,

---

127 *Ibid.*, pp. 82-83. « Eine ottonische Gründung zum hl. Nikolaus ist dann das vor 1005 in Aachen gegründete Kollegiatstift mit einer Kapelle zum hl. Nikolaus, an deren Stelle heute die St. Nikolauspfarrkirche steht. In einer Urkunde Heinrichs II. von 1005, in der das Stift zuerst genannt ist, wird ausdrücklich auch der '*festivitas sancti Nicholai*' Erwähnung getan ».

128 *Ibid.*, p. 83. « ... die im Jahre 1024 durch Pfalzgraf Ezzo gegründet wurde, der Ottos III. Schwester Mathilde zur Gemahlin hatte ».

129 *Ibid.*, pp. 84-85.

Fig. 39. - Aachen-Burtscheid, Church of St. John: *St. Nicholas.* Byzantine mosaic icon, 11th century.

even previous to Nicholas' Translation to Bari in 1087, can most likely be attributed to the Norman seafarers, whose role in acquainting this part of the world with the cult, and nourishing it, cannot be emphasized enough. Nicholas had been their patron well before his relics arrived in Europe; indeed, the church historian Ordericus Vitalis tells us of the time when the most famous Norman of all, William the Conqueror, called upon Nicholas for help during a storm in the English Channel around 1068.[130]

Once in England, the Normans soon took up their patron's cause in the new territory. William himself founded Battle Abbey in Sussex and a subordinate priory cell at Exeter.[131] The latter, dedicated to Nicholas, also owned a Latin manuscript, written about 1087, which contained the saint's legends.[132] While Norman architectural achievements proved of lasting quality in England and France, literary

---

130 *Ibid.*, p. 247. « Ordericus Vitalis berichtet, dass Wilhelm der Eroberer um 1067/68, als er von der Normandie nach England (Winchelsea) überfuhr und in einen Sturm geriet auf die Fürbitte des Heiligen, dessen Festtag die Kirche gerade feierte, wohlbehalten '*ad portum salutis*' gelangte ».

131 W. De Gray Birch, *The Legendary Life of St. Nicholas*, « The Journal of the British Archaeological Association », 42, 1886, 185-204; 44, 1888, 222-234, p. 222. « St. Nicholas of Myra has little or no connection with Battle Abbey; but there was a priory cell or religious house subordinate to Battle, at Exeter, dedicated to St. Nicholas, which, according to the authorities, also owed its foundation to the conqueror. That the Ms. was at an early period in its history connected with Exeter is clear from an insertion, at f. 75, of the text of a spiritual compact made at that city between parties not specially indicated ».

132 *Ibid.*, p. 232. « The manuscript poem is contained among the Cottonian Mss. in the British Museum, Tiberius, B. V. ».

contributions by these northern warriors were found to be equally durable. Concerning the cult, the first non-classical biography of Nicholas was written by the great Norman poet Wace (c 1100-1174), who recorded the legends in Old French during the middle of the twelfth century.[133] This work, in turn, was expanded and translated into Old English by Nicholas Delius.

Throughout Europe, the saint's feast day, December 6, would become a day of festivities during the Middle Ages. Nicholas Day was already noted in France and Germany in the ninth century, but actual celebration evidently did not begin until the middle of the eleventh century. By this time, church texts in Normandy refer to a special mass to Nicholas on December 6,[134] and by the twelfth century other parts of northern France had joined in this observation. The rest of northern Europe would follow a similar pattern: Nicholas Day is mentioned in a missal of Cologne, dated 1133,[135] and in one from Salzburg, dated between 1071 and 1099,[136] while it appears for the first time as a

---

133 MEISEN, p. 217.

134 *Ibid.*, pp. 176-177. « So darf etwa aus dem Vorhandensein des Officiums, das der Mönch Isembert um 1030 in dem Kloster St. Pierre bei Rouen zu Ehren des hl. Nikolaus verfasste, schon eher auf den Festtag des Heiligen, wenn dieser auch vielleicht noch auf das eine Kloster beschränkt blieb, geschlossen werden. Zu diesem verhältnismässig frühen Beleg für die Normandie passt es, und seine Glaubwürdigkeit wird verstärkt, wenn der Geschichtsschreiber der normannischen Kirchengeschichte, Ordericus Vitalis (1075 bis nach 1142), von der kirchlichen Feier des Nikolaustages (6. Dez.) für die Zeit um 1067 und 1068 berichtet ».

135 *Ibid.*, p. 184.

136 *Ibid.*, p. 188.

holiday in Holland in the 1163 festival calendar of St. John in Utrecht.[137]

But let us now turn from the official recording of dates to the more popular and local traditions which manifested themselves in recognition of the saint's feast day. These religious practices, in fact, were firmly woven into the fabric of medieval civilization. One of the more curious customs in northern Europe occurred on December 5, when a boy was elected by his fellow students as Boy Bishop, a role which allowed him to fulfill temporarily the bishop's duties. Nicholas, in one of his many functions, served, of course, as patron of the young, and his association with them will be discussed in greater detail in the following chapter. In another tribute to Nicholas, and for the entertainment and education of the people, special plays were written and performed as part of the Nicholas Day celebration. This is evidenced by a character from a play based on the Deodatus legend, who says « tomorrow will be St. Nicholas' day, whom all Christians should devoutly cherish, venerate and bless, *In crastino erit festivitas Nicolai* ».[138] The quote is taken from a thirteenth century manuscript that once belonged to the Benedictine monastery of Fleury, France, and which now resides in the public library in Orléans.[139]

---

137 *Ibid.*, p. 186.

138 Charles Mills Gayley, *Plays of Our Forefathers, and Some of the Traditions upon Which They Were Founded*, New York, Duffield and Co. 1907, p. 61.

139 Otto E. Albrecht, *Four Latin Plays of St. Nicholas from the 12th Century Fleury Play-Book: Text and Commentary, with a Study of the Music of the Plays, and of the Sources and Icono-*

The Fleury manuscript contained four plays, three of which were based on the vita by Diaconus, and it so happened that a copy of this biography was owned by the monks of Fleury. The fourth play, *The Barbarian and the St. Nicholas Icon*, has been ascribed to Hilarius, who, we should not be surprised to hear, was probably a twelfth century Anglo-Norman.[140] His drama must have held particular appeal for the common people, since it combined the language of the locals, French, with the language of the Church, Latin. A rather amusing translation of this bilingual play can be found with Professor Gayley,[141] and as it seems to capture the mischievous spirit of the medieval choirboys, who most likely also performed it, I would like to share it here with the reader:

His play is well known: a Barbarian (it is from another play that we learn his nationality) who is setting forth on business, entrusts his treasure to the keeping of a shrine of St. Nicholas, ordering the saint, somewhat cavalierly one might say, to see to it that there shall be no cause for complaint upon his return. As soon as the foreigner is out of sight, tramps, *fures transeuntes*, make off with the booty. « Hard luck », cries Barbarus, who had merely stepped round the corner –

Gravis sors et dura!
Hic reliqui plura,
Sed sub mala cura:
Des! Quel domage!
Qui pert la sue chose, purque n'enrage?

---

graphy of the Legends, Philadelphia, University of Pennsylvania Press 1935, p. 1 and p. 5. The Fleury monastery also had a copy of a sermon for St. Nicholas' Day by Hildebert of Le Mans (d. 1139).

140 Gayley, p. 63.

141 *Ibid.*, pp. 63-65.

« I do well to be angry. I left more than a hundred things in charge of this thief of a saint. Ha, Nicholax, if you don't disgorge my chose, you'll catch it ». Then up with his whip –

By God, I swear to you
Unless you « cough up » true,
You thief, I'll beat you blue,
    I will, no fear!
So hand me back my stuff that I put here!

Then St. Nicholas shall go to the robbers and say to them: « Ye wretches, what would you? When you stole the treasure committed to my care, was not I beholding you? Now I have taken a thrashing for them, and my credit is no longer worth a denier. Out with the stolen goods at once:

And if you don't do as I say,
I'll see you both hanged in a day
    On the cross in the square:
Your filching, and fobbing, and face,
Your scandalous deeds of disgrace
    I'll tell to the populace, – there! »

The robbers, fearful, bring back the goods, which when he finds, Barbarus in alternate gasps of Latin and undigested French exclaims, –

Unless my sight deceives me
    I've got them now;
I don't care who believes me,
    'T is marvel still, I vow, –

or words to that effect. He then approaches the image of St. Nicholas, and gives thanks:

Supplex ad te venio
    Nicholax;
Nam per te recipio
Tut icei que tu gardas;

and more. *Beatus Nicholax*, appearing then, bids him give thanks to God alone. And the Barbarian repents of his sins and becomes a Christian, *instanter*, believing that God Almighty, whose kingdom is without end, will blot out his iniquity.

These charming medieval plays might be considered the precursors of modern drama, and those about St. Nicholas were among the finest dramatic presentations. Indeed, they would seem to rival pictorial art in popularizing the saint's life during these early days of the cult in northern Europe.

As we have seen so far, aristocrats and Normans had maintained rather efficient channels of communication between the North and the East. But there was yet another commuter from north of the Alps who, in the course of his travels to or from the East, might have become an adherent of the Nicholas cult. The pilgrim, so characteristic of the Middle Ages, had the opportunity to encounter the saint's numerous disciples and to behold the holy places of worship built to glorify Nicholas' name. Along his burdensome, difficult land route via the Saint Bernard Pass, the medieval pilgrim would find chapels, churches, and cloisters, and – as special enjoyment to the weary – an occasional hospice. A particularly welcome sight may have been the hospice dedicated to St. Nicholas by Bernard of Menthone (d. 1081), after whom the famous Saint Bernard Pass was named.[142] Many a tired pilgrim, grateful for the respite and shelter provided for him high in the forbidding Alps, may have offered his thanks to Nicholas in an evening prayer.

---

[142] Meisen, p. 507.

One traveler who returned with more than mere word about Nicholas was an unknown knight from Lorraine. On his way home from Palestine, he had stopped in 1098 in Bari, where he collected part of a finger of Nicholas.[143] The relic found a resting place, before 1105, in a chapel in Port, on the river Meurthe, near the present day French-German border. Merchants from both countries had anchored their boats in this little riverport for years, but with the newly obtained relic Port soon developed from a tiny marketplace into the largest, most populous town in Lorraine and became known as Saint-Nicolas-du-Port. Its fame increased even more when miracles were reported to take place in this town of pilgrimage. Nicholas by now was revered as the patron of Lorraine, and in order to accommodate the ever growing crowds of pilgrims, a second church had to be constructed. When it proved insufficient, still another church, dedicated in 1193 by Bishop Eudes de Vandemont from Toul, was erected and stood until 1475. Twenty years later, a new pilgrimage church began to rise on the same site, finally completed in 1544 and remaining with us until today. Thus, the acquisition of a small relic transformed an obscure corner of Europe to the most important center north of the Alps for those medieval pilgrims in search of the miraculous powers of St. Nicholas.

So, whether he traveled the sea or pilgrim's routes, moved in the exalted circle of the aristocracy or, more likely, stayed at his humble home, the medieval Christian had a good chance to learn about our venerated saint in story, play or any of the multitude of places dedicated to him.

---

143 *Ibid.*, pp. 515-516.

Before the year 1500, over 2550 such centers existed in western Europe alone, possessing either a church, chapel, cloister, hospice, altar, cemetery, relic or manuscript related to St. Nicholas.[144] They were scattered across the continent in large cities and tiny hamlets, dispersed alongside the rivers that flowed across the fertile plains, and perched upon desolate mountain passes. Through this network the people could keep in constant touch with the saint who had won their hearts and whose cult continued to thrive in the North as a result of their affection. Once settled in his new home in the eleventh century, St. Nicholas and his cult would remain there and steadfastly win converts among successive generations.

The Iconography of Saint Nicholas in Northern Art

In Byzantium Nicholas was presented to the worshipper chiefly through the medium of the icon, in Italy through frescoes and altarpieces, but the media used in northern Europe for the representation of Nicholas were of an almost bewildering variety. Moreover, and in contrast to his Byzantine contemporary, the northern artist did not observe the dictum of a canon, and as a result we find that the diversity of Nicholas' image was as great as the various materials employed by the medieval craftsman to represent him. The cult, deeply imbedded in the life of the people, required an

---

[144] *Ibid.*, pp. 126-176. Meisen lists on these pages all the places by diocese, including their dates; see also the map at the end of the book for their exact geographic location.

abundance of art that would honor the saint and explain his legends. Striving to achieve this end, the medieval painters and sculptors left us a legacy of beautiful art devoted to Nicholas. These artists, working in an environment of religious fervor, made Nicholas one of their leading characters in the drama that unfolded on the creative stage of northern Europe.

The saint's image in Northern art generally lacks a recognizable form or consistent features. Yet, an early twelfth century painted statue (Fig. 40), originally from the abbey church in Brauweiler near Cologne,[145] reveals – uncharacteristically for Northern art – traces of the Byzantine canon. An austere Nicholas, with a lock of hair in the center of a high forehead and a short beard, in this particular case below his jaw, wears a white omophorion decorated with crosses. The reader may recall these elements from the discussion of the iconography of the icon in part I. Nicholas is also shown bareheaded, quite in accordance with Byzantine art but extremely unusual for the product of a northern artist. Although the beard, locally known as *Schifferbart*,[146] does not conform to the true Byzantine canon, the artist appears to have been familiar with Orthodox tradition. Perhaps he even had recourse to the icon in the cloister Burtscheid near Aachen (Fig. 39). The simple lines of the sitting Nicholas, solid in his appearance of quiet dignity, render an impression of granitelike permanence, although the sculptor has carved the figure from wood.

From the same abbey church in Brauweiler comes an-

---

145 *Ibid.*, p. 197.

146 *Ibid.*, p. 197.

other statue of a sitting Nicholas, offering a rather contrasting statement (Fig. 41). The pose may well be alike in both statues, but the movement in the garments and the long, exaggerated fingers of the latter are definitely the expressions of Northern art. This work, executed in 1491, confirms at the same time the survival of the cult over the centuries as well as the elimination of all iconographic influence from Byzantium. The twelfth century statue with its resemblance to Nicholas' Byzantine image, though modified by the German artist, was really quite unique for this period, and the absence of other works in this style by northern painters and sculptors seems to indicate that they rejected the Byzantine image of Nicholas from an early date on in preference to their own regional interpretations of the saint and his legends.

Nicholas' popularity assured him a secure place in the decoration of the great cathedrals as well as of the lesser known religious institutions in the North. At Chartres he appears seven times, either in the stained glass windows or in stone carvings.[147] In the entrance of the south portal he stands to the right of St. Leo and St. Ambrose, a position of such prominence that he was sure to be noticed by the throngs of people who came to worship at Chartres. Like the other figures, Nicholas, erect as a column, forms a strong vertical in submission to the demands of the Gothic architecture. The stone has been finely carved with accurate

---

[147] EMILE MÂLE, *Religious Art in France, XIII Century. A Study in Mediaeval Iconography and Its Sources of Inspiration*, trans. from the third edition by Dora Nussy, London, J. M. Dent & Sons, Ltd. 1913, p. 328.

details; yet, without any striking individual features the saint's identity remains almost obscure.

One sure way to eliminate this sense of anonymity would be to display Nicholas with one or more of his symbols. In Italy we saw how he often carried three golden spheres, and in Germany he was at times shown holding three golden apples, three stones or three loaves of bread,[148] all symbols which were directly derived from the legends of *The Three Destitute Maidens* and *The Miracle of the Corn Ships*. By far the most popular attribute attached to the saint in France symbolizes the legend of *St. Nicholas As He Resuscitates Three Dead Students*, a story already described in Part II.[149] The symbol of three nude boys in a tub is well exhibited in a statue by Jan Hans (Fig. 42), dated 1708, and located in the church of St. Nicolas-outre-Meuse in Liège.[150] Nicholas certainly cuts a dramatic figure in his swirling garments, and his identity is unmistakably clarified by the attribute at his feet. A twelfth century miracle play is the oldest extant form of this legend,[151] which was invented in northern France in order to widen Nicholas' patronage of young women to include the protection of young men who traveled across France to Europe's best medieval schools.

Just as the bishop of Myra was able to take his place

---

148 MEISEN, pp. 209-211.

149 See Part II of this book for a discussion of the legend as it appears on the stone relief in the St. Nicholas church in Bari (Fig. 12).

150 MEISEN, p. 310.

151 *Ibid.*, p. 289.

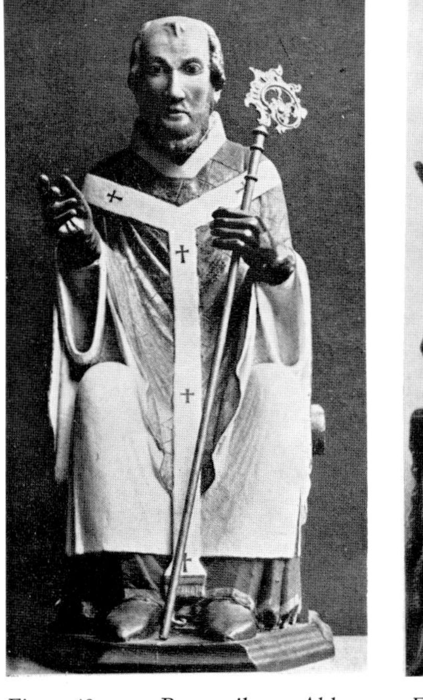

Fig. 40. - Brauweiler, Abbey Church, near Cologne: *St. Nicholas.* Wood statue, 12th century.

Fig. 41. - Brauweiler, Abbey Church, near Cologne: *St. Nicholas.* Statue, 1491.

Fig. 42. - JAN HANS: *St. Nicholas and the Three Resuscitated Students*, Liège, Church of St. Nicolas-outre-Meuse. Statue, 1709.

alongside other saints before large congregations in the great public churches of Europe, so, too, was he allowed to enter the private world of the Book of Hours. The best of these books were usually produced for a great lord or his lady, artistic treasures which remained in their families for generations. In two of the very finest manuscripts Nicholas has been assigned his own page. The first book was painted by an artist known only as the « Master of the Hours of the Maréchal de Boucicaut » or the « Boucicaut Master ». Since there are no records to disclose any information about the illuminator, he has been named after the pious adventurer for whom his bestknown work was painted. The patron, Jean II le Meingre, simply called Boucicaut, had been appointed Marshal of France in 1391 by King Charles VI inspite of his bourgeois origin. In 1393, Marshal Boucicaut won the hand of Antoinette de Turenne, but only after the intervention of King Charles and others had overcome the opposition of Antoinette's father. Marshal Boucicaut, Christian knight he was, fought against the Turks and, though very nearly decapitated after the battle of Nicopolis in 1396, returned two years later to the fight in which he helped to save Constantinople. Chivalrous knight as well as warrior, he founded an order in 1399 for the protection of noble ladies in distress, the « ordre de la dame blanche à l'écu vert ».[152] Boucicaut was captured in 1415 at Agincourt and died, while still a captive, in England in 1421.

---

[152] MILLARD MEISS, *French Painting in the Time of Jean de Berry. The Boucicaut Master*, London, Phaidon 1968, p. 9.

The exact date of the manuscript is in doubt, but it was painted in Paris during the first decade of the fifteenth century,[153] and now resides in the Musée Jacquemart-André in Paris. There are forty-one miniatures in this Book of Hours, twenty-seven of them full page paintings of saints, and one of them is devoted to St. Nicholas (Fig. 43). Given the history of the Marshal, one might assume that a scene from the *Stratelates* or *The Three Destitute Maidens* would have been an appropriate choice. Instead, the saint is again clearly associated with the legend *St. Nicholas Resuscitates Three Dead Students*, as is indicated by the three nude boys emerging from the barrel. Perhaps the illuminator felt that this was the better established symbol of Nicholas in France. The family coat of arms in the background should not distract us from acknowledging the more technical achievements of the Boucicaut Master. His realistic treatment of space in the receding floor tiles and in the curving lines of the barrel can still be appreciated in a composition
lines of the barrel can still be appreciated in a composition, which is very much confined to the foreground. As customary, Nicholas wears his complete bishop's regalia; nevertheless, the Boucicaut Master has managed to project a warm, naturalistic saint.

The second manuscript, more famous than the *Boucicaut Hours*, is the *Belles Heures of Jean, Duke of Berry*, now to be found in the Cloisters Collection of the Met-

---

[153] ERWIN PANOFSKY, *Early Netherlandish Painting, Its Origins and Character*, 2 vol., New York, Icon Editions 1971, 1: 55. Panofsky believes that the Boucicaut Master painted this book on and off between 1400 and 1411. - MEISS, *Boucicaut Master*, p. 132. But Meiss says that the most likely date seems 1405-08.

Fig. 43. - Paris, Musée Jaquemart-André: *St. Nicholas and the Three Resuscitated Students.* The Hours of the Maréchal de Boucicaut, Ms. 2, fol. 33*v*, c. 1405-08.

ropolitan Museum of Art, New York. The *Belles Heures* was painted about 1408-10 by the Limbourg brothers, the most wonderful trio of illuminators in Northern art. A full page in this manuscript has been dedicated to the scene *St. Nicholas Saves Seafarers from Shipwreck* (Fig. 44). The Limbourgs earned a reputation as exquisite painters of beautiful landscapes, and this seascape with Nicholas certainly equals the quality of their rendition of the four seasons. According to Meiss, the artist of the seascape was Herman Limbourg,[154] who proves himself a master of atmospheric effects in the application of light and dark blue sky and a touch of grey storm clouds. Urgent movement is suggested by the short, energetic lines of the sea's turbulent waves in which the ship flounders. A supernatural Nicholas in a flowing, golden robe has arrived just in time to grasp the broken mast and to save the desperate crew. This composition could be based on an Italian model,[155] but Herman injects a northern feeling for the moods of nature.

On occasion, Nicholas' posthumous influence was felt by the populace from birth to death, just as when he performed baptisms and last rites during his lifetime as the bishop of Myra. Centuries later, among the many different places protected by the saint were also the final resting places of Christians. Such a cemetery was consecrated to

---

[154] MILLARD MEISS and ELIZABETH H. BEATSON, *The Belles Heures of Jean, Duke of Berry*, New York, George Braziller 1974, folio 168.

[155] MEISS, *Belles Heures*, folio 168. « Perhaps the Limbourgs had seen the fresco in San Francesco, Siena, in which Ambrogio Lorenzetti, Ghiberti tells us, painted a severe storm ».

Fig. 44. - New York, Cloisters Collection of the Metropolitan Museum of Art: *St. Nicholas Saves Seafarers in a Storm.* Les Belles Heures du Duc de Berry, fol. 168, 1408-10.

Nicholas on March 11, 1096, by Pope Urban II near Tours.[156] At the beginning of life's Christian journey, the saint could again be present, this time as witness to a baptism. At Tournai, in modern day Belgium, baptismal fonts – some of them decorated with St. Nicholas legends – were produced and exported to other parts of Europe. Two of these Romanesque fonts found their way to Zedelghem, near Bruges, and to Winchester Cathedral in England. The Zedelghem font (Fig. 45) displays on one side St. Nicholas as he revives the three dead students; in a peculiar way, the boys seem to be wrapped up like Egyptian mummies. Obviously the symbol of the three children in a tub had not yet been developed. The Winchester font (Fig. 46) reproduces the same scene in an even more compressed form, for the Roman columns and arches of the Zedelghem font are missing. The font at Winchester has been dated c 1150,[157] close to the time when the story originated in France. Both these twelfth century fonts are primitive carvings without depth. Their short, squat, large-headed figures in a scene with few details set no real iconographic precedent for later artists. To choose this particular legend for the baptismal ceremony was to remind the parents of Nicholas' patronage of the young, and we find the same legend in the Cathedral of Freiburg, Switzerland, where

---

[156] MEISEN, pp. 511-512. « Einen Monat später, am 11. März 1096, weihte Urban II. dann in dem benachbarten Tours einen Friedhof zu Ehren des hl. Nikolaus ».

[157] EDWARD S. PRIOR and ARTHUR GARDINAR, *An Account of Medieval Figure-Sculpture in England*, 2 vols., Cambridge, Cambridge University Press 1912, 1: 203.

Fig. 45. - Zedelghem, Belgium: *St. Nicholas Resuscitates Three Students.* Relie sculpture, baptismal font, 12th century.

Fig. 46. - Winchester Cathedral: Relief sculpture, baptismal font, c. 1150.

it is carved in the choir stalls (Fig. 47), once again close to young people and probably to the enjoyment of the boys who sang there.

So far, we have encountered representations of St. Nicholas in wood, stone and vellum, but his stories were also reproduced in glass and embellished many a stained glass window in the medieval churches of western Europe. Emile Mâle, writing about occurrences in France, informs us: [158]

> At Chartres, where the work is practically complete, St. Nicholas is painted or carved no less than seven times, and the very incomplete windows at Auxerre, like those at Le Mans, tell his legend twice. It is found again in the cathedrals of Rouen, Bourges and Tours, in St. Julien-du-Sault in Burgundy and in St. Remi at Reims ... In a word, St. Nicholas is almost always met with where windows of the 13th century still exist.

We shall look at only one of those windows, located in Bourges Cathedral, since the others do not deviate appreciably from its Gothic style.

The Nicholas window at Bourges (Fig. 48) tells four of his legends in three lights, reading from bottom to top: *The Three Resuscitated Students*; *The Three Destitute Maidens*; three scenes from the *Stratelates*; and finally, the story of *The Boy with the Golden Goblet Who Fell into the Sea.* In the analysis of the bottom roundel, we come across an odd pairing of legends – one violent, the other peaceful. Though they both present Nicholas as patron of the young, the stories are truly opposites in content,

---

[158] MÂLE, *Religious Art in France*, pp. 328-329.

Fig. 47. - Freiburg Cathedral, Switzerland: *St. Nicholas Resuscitates Three Students*. Relief sculpture, choir.

Fig. 48. - Bourges Cathedral: *Scenes From the Legends of St. Nicholas.* Stained glass window, 13th century.

with the three students to become unwitting murder victims of the innkeeper and the three slumbering maidens about to be rewarded by Nicholas. Yet, the artist manages to unite them both pictorially in his similar alignment of sleeping bodies and by applying the same color scheme, red, green and gold, to the sheets in which they are wrapped. On the theory that this repetition would better balance these diverse dramas, the medieval master creates a harmonious unit of the window as a whole.

The scenes from the three *Stratelates* begin at the bottom of the middle roundel, where the generals are shown as they are brought before Constantine on false charges. On the next level, we see them in jail and the moment when Nicholas admonishes the emperor to free the innocent men. The story concludes on the bottom section of the top roundel: Constantine sends the *Stratelates* with gifts to Myra. Like the two previous legends, the episode has been narrated with detail in colorful scenes.

As we come to the summit of the window, we meet a legend which has yet to be discussed. A noble couple prayed to Nicholas to fulfill their fervent wish for a son, and the husband promised to make a pilgrimage to Myra, where he would place a golden goblet at the saint's tomb. When the son was born and had grown up, the time arrived to visit Myra. But the specially commissioned gold goblet had turned out to be so beautiful that the father decided to keep it for his own use, ordering a copy for the saint instead. During the voyage, the boy fell overboard with the original goblet and drowned. The bereaved father completed the journey alone and placed the copy on Nicholas' altar. Strangely enough, the copy fell off at once, and so the father tried to put it back. The golden cup, however, fell down a second time, and while the father pondered this odd happening, his son suddenly appeared, sound and well, with the original goblet in his hand. Overjoyed, the parent donated the original cup as well as the copy to Nicholas.[159]

Although these grateful pilgrims are going to Myra, this legend originated after 1087 in northern France.[160] We can follow the storyline at the top of the Bourges window from left to right. The opening scene shows the boy, who still holds the goblet, as he is pulled into the sea by a small, blue devil with wings and a red face, while the father watches helplessly from a ship which resembles in type those used by the Vikings. Now the artist proceeds directly to the closing moments of the legend. The parents kneel before the altar upon which a gold cup has been placed; Nicholas and the boy, clasping the original goblet, stand immediately behind them in the prominent center frame. Again the artist describes the high points with lucidity, although he reduces buildings to mere architectural symbolism, much like a Byzantine painter would. To me, however, the French artist draws a more natural figure and gives a better account of the stories through his carefully chosen narrative.

Across the border, German painters were no less attracted by Nicholas' life as a theme for their designs in stained glass windows. In the cathedral of Freiburg im

---

[159] JACOBUS, p. 23. - MEISEN, pp. 276-277.

[160] MEISEN, p. 277. - BIRCH, p. 232. The legend can be found in the Cottonian Mss. in the British Museum, Tiberius, B. V., dated c. 1087.

Breisgau, two of the four windows, called the *Tulenhaupt-fenster*, depict four of the Nicholas legends. These windows, dated about 1320-30,[161] were named after the local Tulenhaupt family whose coat of arms we see twice in the two central windows, once underneath the Virgin and again below the Apostle with a cross.[162] The presence of the coat of arms reassures us that at least these two windows were donated by the Tulenhaupts, whereas it remains doubtful whether the two Nicholas windows were also commissioned by the same family. A clue to the donor of these two windows may lie in the word *Dieselmuot*, which is written across the very bottom under small scenes composed of little, white-clad figures, chipping away with hammers at the surrounding rock. *Dieselmuot* was the name of a silver mine on the mountain *Schauinsland* near Freiburg,[163] and it stands to reason that these busy figures represent the miners whose guild most likely contributed the Nicholas windows to the cathedral.

The familiar Byzantine legend of *The Three Destitute Maidens* was selected to decorate the top portion of the

---

161 INGEBORG KRUMMER-SCHROTH, *Glasmalereien aus dem Freiburger Münster*, Freiburg im Breisgau, Rombach 1967, p. 110. « ... dass das Tulenhauptfenster um 1320/30 gemalt wurde ... ».

162 *Ibid.*, p. 98. « ... das Fenster über dem südlichen Seitenschiffportal (Nr. 8), dessen vier Bahnen durch den Portaleinbau etwas kürzer sind als die übrigen, hat seinen Namen nach der Familie Tulenhaupt, deren Wappen in den beiden Mittellanzetten zu finden ist. Ein Lindenbaum (tilia) auf einem grünen Dreiberg vor goldenem gemustertem Rautengrund des Schildes weist auf die Familie hin ».

163 *Ibid.*, p. 104. « Unter den Darstellungen ist ein Schriftband mit dem Wort Dieselmout. Dies war der Name einer Grube auf dem Berg Schauinsland bei Freiburg ... ».

left window (Fig. 49). In contrast to the Bourges painting, the maidens step eagerly forward to accept their dowry. The scene below presents the relatively new northern legend in which St. Nicholas restores three students to life. Omitted is the wicked act of the innkeeper, but we notice an unusual addition: a hand in a golden halo near Nicholas' head, signifying the intervention of God.

The top of the right window (Fig. 50) tells in a single composition the western story of the Nicholas picture that protected the Jew's treasure. Earlier, this legend was referred to as *The Barbarian and the St. Nicholas Icon*, and the reader may recall the entertaining account from the Fleury manuscript, translated by Professor Gayley. But in this stained glass rendition, the barbarian in the literary event has been replaced by a gentleman, identified by his hat as a Jew.[164] The captured moment is the one in which the Jewish owner of the stolen property threatens the Nicholas painting with his stick; the act does not deter the thief, who marches off with the goods. Missing is the later part of the story, where the saint forces the thieves to return the treasure to its rightful owner. In the center portion of the same window we once again come upon an old and famous Byzantine legend, *St. Nicholas As He Saves a Ship in a Storm.* Throwing his decorum temporarily aside, Nicholas protects his mariners in a most imaginative manner by attacking the *Windteufel* (Wind Devil) directly with his bishop's crozier. What a difference in approach between

---

[164] *Ibid.*, p. 103. The owner of the treasure wears a Jewish hat. « ... Links haut der Jude, in grünem Kleid und rotem Mantel mit dem weissen Judenhut gekleidet, mit dem Stock auf das Bild ein ... ».

Fig. 49. - Freiburg im Breisgau Cathedral: The left Tulenhaupwindow. Stained glass window, c. 1320-30.

Fig. 50. - Freiburg im Breisgau Cathedral: The right Tulenhauptwindow. Stained glass window, c. 1320-30.

the artist of this work and Herman Limbourg's later painting of the same legend in the *Belles Heures* (Fig. 44)! Herman employed atmospheric effects for his description of the storm at sea, but the German medieval painter used the symbolism of a black devil on a white sail, twisted around the mast, to portray the same hazardous situation. I find this scene in stained glass from the cathedral of Freiburg im Breisgau to be the most amusing and charming in the entire Nicholas repertoire.

Seen as a whole, the Nicholas windows in Freiburg, with their oak leaf borders and golden-framed scenes, form a wonderfully geometric and symbolic rather than narrative design, as is the case in Bourges. What the layouts of the Nicholas windows in both cathedrals do have in common is the artists' alternation of old Byzantine with newer western legends, surely not an accidental arrangement. These medieval stained glass windows were an excellent medium of communication, especially when enhanced by the truly heavenly light streaming through their many colorful facets towards the receptive worshippers in the church below.

Now let us retrace our steps and examine a few Nicholas windows in England. The legends, of course, were known there through the Normans, and the story depicted on the thirteenth century window in the Jerusalem Chamber of Westminster Abbey, *The Boy and the Gold Goblet*,[165] was contained in the already mentioned Latin manuscript, once owned by the religious house in Exeter. To our misfortune, the Westminster Abbey window (Fig. 51) has deteriorated

---

165 John Baker, *English Stained Glass*, introduction by Herbert Read, London, Thames and Hudson 1960, p. 56.

Fig. 51. - Westminster Abbey, Jerusalem Chamber: *St. Nicholas and the Boy with the Gold Goblet.* Stained glass window, north window, 13th century.

to such an extent that the picture is blurred and hard to read. But we can again distinguish a Viking-like ship from which the boy has fallen into the water. Here St. Nicholas acts promptly; dressed in his bishop's robes and miter and carrying his crozier, he rises from the waves at the prow of the ship to rescue the boy. We are treated to a more realistic composition in a much later version of the same legend (Fig. 52), which appears in a sixteenth century window panel of the Hillesden Church in Buckinghamshire.[166] A closer look aboard ship, where the crew struggles with the ropes attached to the billowing sails, discloses sixteenth century clarity and naturalism.

One of Nicholas' less savory associations, as we know from the twelfth century play by Hilarius, was with thieves. His patronage of robbers developed mainly from legends such as *The Jew and the Cheating Christian*, and *The Jew Who Owned a St. Nicholas Icon*. Though the latter legend originated neither in the North nor in the East but in Calabria around 1000,[167] it seemed to hold a certain attraction for the North, at least from the time of the Fleury plays. During Elizabethan days, thieves were sometimes referred to as « St. Nicholas' clerks ». In the *First Part of King Henry IV*, act II, scene 2, Shakespeare writes:

Gadshill: « Sirrah, if they meet not with Saint Nicholas' clerks, I'll give thee this neck ».

---

166 *Ibid.*, p. 218.

167 ANRICH, 2: 430. Anrich believes that it originated in Calabria about 1000. - MEISEN, pp. 261-263. Originally it was a Vandal who owned a Nicholas picture. Later it became a Jew. - JACOBUS, pp. 22-23. Jacobus writes that a Jew owns a statue of St. Nicholas.

Fig. 52. - Hillesden Church, Buckinghamshire: *St. Nicholas and the Boy with the Gold Goblet.* Stained glass window, east window, 16th century.

Chamberlain: « No, I'll none of it: I prithee, keep that for the hangman; for I know thou worshippest Saint Nicholas as truly as a man of falsehood may ».

Characters of such ill repute can be met in Hillesden Church in other Nicholas window panels that deal with the legend of *The Jew Who Owned a St. Nicholas Icon.* Brazenly, the robbers steal the treasure right from under Nicholas' eyes, and in gleeful anticipation they lift the lid of the moneybox (Fig. 53). In the next light of the window, the disappointed guardian confronts some of his dishonest charges, instructing them to return the stolen goods. Faith eventually triumphs in the last scene, when Nicholas' « clerks » restore the property to its thankful Jewish owner (Fig. 54).

The art of Flanders may very well have been the source for the finely drawn, convincing characterizations in these English stained glass windows. The roughly hewn features of the robbers bring to mind the Flemish peasants of Pieter Bruegel the Elder, so typically exemplified in his *Peasant Dance.* But whatever the roots, the painter of the Hillesden Nicholas window produced an entertaining experience for the viewers. This pictorial narrative in stained glass vividly complements the written account of the same legend by Hilarius in the twelfth century Fleury manuscript.

Our esteemed Nicholas, simultaneously serving as patron of rich merchants and the thieves who robbed them, was an extraordinary saint indeed, a man for all the people. The development of his cult in western Europe, and elsewhere, crossed all class, social, age, and time barriers, and his enormous popularity is quickly supported by the great

Fig. 53. - Hillesden Church, Buckinghamshire: *The Jew and the St. Nicholas Picture.* Detail of robbers. Stained glass window, 16th century.

number of architectural and artistic works dedicated to him. In this chapter, I have sought to illustrate to some extent how Nicholas themes abounded in a diversity of media and locale, giving an indication of the saint's true involvement in European civilization. In art, the representation of his legends may have adjusted to the style of each period, but his deeds and miracles never ceased to be an inspiration to northern creativity. An assessment of Nicholas' iconography in Northern art leaves us with only one outstanding, consistent element, one that stresses his position in the hierarchy of the Church. He almost always appears dressed in his complete liturgical regalia: the bishop's robe, miter, and crozier. Carrying his staff, the bishop of Myra is never more the shepherd of his flock than when he rises from the sea to save a boy or flies through the air to rescue mariners in distress. The miraculous aspect of most of his legends held a magnetic fascination for the artists of northern Europe, at least until the Reformation. After Luther, when the appeal of saints slowly diminished, Nicholas' religious role also declined. But wherever the cult of saints continued to be celebrated over the centuries, St. Nicholas retained his medieval dignity and authoritative demeanor in Northern art.

Fig. 54. - Hillesden Church, Buckinghamshire: *The Robbers Return the Stolen Goods to the Jew.* Stained glass window, 16th century.

Part Four

SAINT NICHOLAS' TRANSFORMATION IN AMERICA

Saint Nicholas and the Christmas Celebration

At last, the end of our long pilgrimage is in sight as we approach the skyline of New York. It was here, in the nineteenth century, that the august saint of the Middle Ages was recreated in literature and art to become the jolly, portly St. Nicholas who arrives late on Christmas Eve to the enchantment of young and old. A New York writer recorded the mythical appearance of a gift-bearing Nicholas on the night before Christmas in a poem of everlasting fame, and several years later this lovable character was brought to visual life by an artist who resided in the same city. We owe it mostly to the combined talents of these two men that St. Nicholas became so much a part of the traditional Christmas as we know it in America. And even though the final metamorphosis from Saint Nicholas to Santa Claus took place in the New World, the ultimate source for this transformation lay deep within the history of the Old World.

December had been a month of festivals long before the days of Christianity. One of the most important of these pagan festivities, for instance, the Roman Saturnalia, occurred between December 17 and December 23. We should also remember that the Germanic tribes in the North were not fully converted to the Christian faith until the rule of Charlemagne (742?-814) and that some of the heathen traditions lingered into the new era. The Christian calendar, in turn, set aside the last month of the year for the observation of a number of holy days, including, of course, Christ's birthday on December 25 and Nicholas' feast day on December 6. How Nicholas joined the later and unrelated Christmas celebration shall be the subject under discussion in this chapter.

It was during the Middle Ages and as patron of students that Nicholas first gained entrance to the Christmas season. The participation of young men from December 25 to December 28 in the so-called Festival of Fools, a derivative of the Saturnalia, the animal masquerade of the Celts, and the Oriental King of Fools,[168] had shed disrepute unto the students for their unruly and unreligious behavior. As a consequence, this frivolous event was replaced by the Students' Festival, celebrated on December 28, Holy Innocents Day. Monk Ekkehard (c 980-1060), delighted with the seriousness of the new holiday, shared his impressions in a report about the visit of King Conrad I to the monastery in St. Gall at Christmas time in 912:

It would be a long story to tell what pleasure he had by day and night, especially in the procession of children; and he was

---

168 Meisen, pp. 307-308.

amazed at their discipline, for though he had ordered that apples should be strewn before them down the middle of the aisle, not even the tiniest lad broke ranks or stretched his hand out to get one.[169]

To hold the young people's anniversary on the day of commemoration for the innocent children killed by Herod of Ascalon seemed quite natural, and to include the children's own patron in this holy day strikes us as equally logical. Our first written evidence on Nicholas' involvement in the Students' Festival at Holy Innocents comes from a thirteenth century Ordinarius of the Cathedral of Bayeux. According to an edict, the *processio infantium*, the procession of children led by the Boy Bishop, stopped on the evening of December 27 before the altar of St. Nicholas and sang a lesson about the saint.[170] The Boy Bishop, who was elected on December 5, did not perform his bishop's duties until Holy Innocents, and in some German communities the students' celebration, which started with the election of the Boy Bishop, would soon last the entire three weeks until December 28.[171] Perhaps as a result of

---

169 GAYLEY, p. 55. - MEISEN, pp. 310-311. Meisen also reports the same visit.

170 MEISEN, p. 318. « Als Zeugnis für die beginnende Verschiebung der Feier von der ursprünglichen Festzeit am Tag der Unschuldigen Kinder auf den Tag des hl. Nikolaus mag man eine Bestimmung im Ordinarius der Kathedrale von Bayeux, der dem 13. Jahrhundert entstammt, ansehen, nach der am Vorabend des Tages der Unschuldigen Kinder im Anschlusse an die Vesper eine Prozession der Chorknaben zum Altare des hl. Nikolaus vorgeschrieben wurde ».

171 MEISEN, p. 324. « In Lübeck dauerte das Bischofsspiel im Anfange des 14. Jahrhunderts vom 6. bis 28. Dezember, also volle

this unusually long interruption to the students' studies, the festival was moved forward in Germany in the fourteenth century to December 6. During the same century, December 6 was marked in the Netherlands by a free school day and gifts of food and money for the pupils. But once again some of the excesses of the Fools' Festival crept back into their festive activities, and the enthusiasm and the high spirited pranks of the boys eventually would draw renewed protests from the older, outraged citizens.

A prominent critic of these extravagancies was Martin Luther. He pronounced in no uncertain terms that the Boy Bishop and his masqueraders would not be recognized by God.[172] The new Protestant religion, of course, sought to remove the cult of all saints, not only the worship of St. Nicholas. Due to his exceptional popularity, however, the bishop of Myra had to be viewed in a different light, and even Luther, whose own family practiced the custom of presenting gifts on Nicholas Day,[173] could not overlook the saint's favored position in the traditions of the land. Recognizing the impossibility of divorcing Nicholas from the common people, he allowed for a continuation of the festival, though he believed it contained childish things and

---

drei Wochen, wie das aus einem Statut des Bischofs Heinrich von Lübeck vom Jahre 1336 hervorgeht ».

172 *Ibid.*, p. 328. « ... konnte Luther den Ausspruch tun: ' Denn Gott kennet das Larvenvolk und Niclas Bischoffe nicht, sintemal sie nicht lehren, noch einigs bischofflichs Ampts pflegen ' ».

173 *Ibid.*, p. 469. « Bereits bei Luther, der selbst, wie oben nachgewiesen wurde, in seiner Familie den Nikolausbrauch noch übte... ».

occasional lies.[174] Yet from this point in time, while Nicholas remained as revered a saint as ever in the Catholic Church, he gradually began to lose his religious quality in the Protestant areas where he was now primarily seen as the dispenser of gifts.

The custom of giving small presents, like sweets and fruit, to good children in Nicholas' name also began during the Middle Ages. At times, an adult, dressed as St. Nicholas and accompanied by a helper, brought the gifts in a sack on the eve or the morning of December 6.[175] To this day the practice prevails, hardly unchanged, in the Catholic parts of Germany, Switzerland, northern France, Belgium, and even Protestant Holland.[176] The impersonation of Nich-

---

[174] *Ibid.*, p. 469. « ' Die Legend des heutigen Festes, des heiligen Bischofs Nicolai, wollen wir lassen anstehen, denn sie viel kindische Dinge und zu Zeiten auch Lügen mit einmischet ' ... ».

[175] *Ibid.*, p. 23. « Im katholischen deutschen Westen und Süden wird heute der Brauch, wenn man von einigen nebensächlichen Umständen absieht, im wesentlichen wie folgt geübt: Am Vorabend oder am Morgen des Nikolaustages (6. Dezember) werden die Kinder mit Gaben (Äpfeln, Nüssen, Leckereien, Gebrauchsgegenständen usw.) beschert, indem ihnen gesagt wird, dass der hl. Nikolaus sie den artigen und fleissigen Kindern gebracht habe, unartige und in der Schule und im Hause träge Kinder erhalten statt der das Kinderherz erfreuenden Dinge eine Rute oder einen Stock. Findet die Kinderbescherung schon am Vorabend des 6. Dezembers statt, so erscheint sehr häufig der Nikolaus selbst, in den sich ein Erwachsener verkleidet hat, entweder allein oder in Begleitung einer dienenden Gestalt, die Gaben, Rute, Sack usw. trägt. Nikolaus teilt dann an die artigen unter ihnen seine Gaben aus, während der Begleiter, der je nach der Landschaft einen verschiedenen Namen führt, mit der Rute oder dem Sacke droht ».

[176] *Ibid.*, p. 22. « In der Tat lässt sich zeigen, dass die heutige Gepflogenheit in den stets katholisch gebliebenen Teilen Deutschlands, in der Schweiz, in Nordfrankreich, Belgien und sogar in den

olas in the home might very well have been inspired by the medieval miracle plays where the part of Nicholas was enacted on the eve of his feast day. In addition, the custom offered an excellent chance to impart an educational lesson, for only worthy boys and girls were rewarded while the lazy and naughty youngsters received a stick or rod from the newly acquired, mean companion of the saint. Since it would have been quite out of character for the loving, forgiving and longstanding protector of the young to perform any act but a benevolent one, medieval folklore invented this threatening figure to serve as a counterpoint to the noble and kind St. Nicholas. Thus, the task of chastising bad children fell to the devil-like assistant whose existence would take on a new importance after the Reformation.

Once the status of saints had been all but eliminated in the converted regions of Europe, Nicholas' helper gained in prominence and slowly eased out the saint in the Protestant areas of Germany. This previously coarse and feared individual gradually assimilated some of the saint's refined qualities and ultimately assumed his role as bestower of gifts. By no means, however, did this new composite figure emerge everywhere with a singular identity. Instead, almost each Protestant pocket seemed to cherish its own version of the saint's replacement. And there was yet another adjustment in the traditional observance of the custom: in the course of time, and depending on the character and his region, the gift giving was sometimes performed on Christmas Eve rather than on St. Nicholas' feast day, a reflection

---

protestantischen Niederlanden mit dem allgemein üblichen Brauch um 1500 in allen wesentlichen Merkmalen übereinstimmt ».

on the Protestant philosophy that all good things radiate from Christ.[177]

One result of the regional variables was a kaleidoscope of names, usually a derivative of the name Nicholas. In the Rhine province, to cite just one example, Nicholas' former companion became known after the Reformation as Pelznickel. He was described as a man with a long, dark beard, heavy boots, often wearing a fur coat or fur hat, and carrying a heavy stick and a sack, partially filled with ashes.[178] The description neatly fitted the earlier medieval figure, but his reformed character was clearly announced by his name which combined features of the old and the new: Pelz referred to the Pelzmantel – or fur coat – he wore, and nickel was simply a shorter form of Nicholas. In this particular region of Germany, then, St. Nicholas in his exquisite bishop's robes was finally superseded as bringer of gifts by a sack-toting Pelznickel, dressed in a fur coat and cap.

---

[177] *Ibid.*, p. 472. « Im ersteren Falle entstand eine Figur, deren Hauptaufgabe die Austeilung von Geschenken wurde, und die man, um auch darin den durch die Reformation geschaffenen veränderten Verhältnissen Rechnung zu tragen, nicht mehr am Vorabende des Festtages des hl. Nikolaus, sondern am Weihnachtsabende erscheinen liess, weil man glaubte, den Kindern zeigen zu müssen, dass alles Gute auf Erden nicht von den Heiligen, sondern vom ' Christ ' selbst käme. So wurde aus dem mittelalterlichen gabenspendenden Nikolaus der Weihnachtsmann der protestantischen Gegenden ... ».

[178] *Ibid.*, p. 471. « Auf die Frage nach dem Aussehen wurde in der Rheinprovinz angegeben: langer dunkler Bart, schwere Stiefel, dunkler langer Mantel, oft Pelzmantel mit Kapuze oder Pelzmütze, auch schwarze Mütze, schwerer Stock, auch wohl Besen, Sack, zum Teil mit Asche gefüllt oder auch mit heraushängenden Beinen, zum Zeichen, dass schon ein unartiger Junge in dem Sack steckte, der mitgenommen wurde, usw ».

Now we must hasten on across the Atlantic Ocean to look at the American variant of this new St. Nicholas. He arrived at the shores of the New World as part of the cultural possessions of the many immigrants who came from northern Europe. A man by the name of Clement C. Moore took the Protestant conception of this friendly visitor to children and made him the subject of a poem so popular and influential that it would establish the iconography of St. Nicholas, the gift giver, in America.[179] Born in New York on July 15, 1779, Moore, the son of a clergyman, graduated from Columbia at the age of nineteen, first in his class, and went on to become a respected scholar in his home town.[180] While he lived in Chelsea, he wrote his famous account of Christmas Eve, titled *A Visit From St. Nicholas*, probably as a surprise for his small children:

'T was the night before Christmas, when all through the house,
Not a creature was stirring, not even a mouse;
The stockings were hung by the chimney with care,
In hopes that St. Nicholas soon would be there;
The children were nestled all snug in their beds,
While visions of sugar-plums danced in their heads;
And Mamma in her 'kerchief, and I in my cap,
Had just settled our brains for a long winter's nap;
When out on the lawn there arose such a clatter,

---

[179] I have ignored St. Nicholas' eight tiny reindeer, his sleigh and the tradition of hanging up stockings on Christmas Eve in order to concentrate on the iconography of the Santa Claus figure.

[180] CLEMENT C. MOORE, *A Visit From St. Nicholas.* Facsimiles of the Earliest Printed Newspaper and Pamphlet Versions and a Halograph Manuscript with a Commentary by Clifton Fadiman, New York, Giniger 1967, pp. 11-13.

I spang from the bed to see what was the matter.
Away to the window I flew like a flash,
Tore open the shutters and threw up the sash.
The moon, on the breast of the new-fallen snow,
Gave the lustre of mid-day to objects below,
When, what to my wondering eyes should appear,
But a miniature sleigh, and eight tiny rein-deer,
With a little old driver, so lively and quick,
I knew in a moment it must be St. Nick.
More rapid than eagles his coursers they came,
And he whistled, and shouted, and called them by name;
« Now, *Dasher*! now, *Dancer*! now, *Prancer* and *Vixen*!
On, *Comet*! on, *Cupid*! on, *Donder* and *Blitzen*!
To the top of the porch! to the top of the wall!
Now dash away! dash away! dash away all! »
As dry leaves that before the wild hurricane fly,
When they meet with an obstacle, mount to the sky;
So up to the house-top the coursers they flew,
With the sleigh full of Toys, and St. Nicholas too.
And then in a twinkling, I heard on the roof,
The prancing and pawning of each little hoof –
As I drew in my head, and was turning around,
Down the chimney St. Nicholas came with a bound.
He was dressed all in fur, from his head to his foot,
And his clothes were all tarnished with ashes and soot;
A bundle of Toys he had flung on his back,
And he looked like a pedlar just opening his pack.
His eyes–how they twinkled! his dimples, how merry!
His cheeks were like roses, his nose like a cherry!
His droll little mouth was drawn up like a bow,
And the beard of his chin was as white as the snow;
The stump of a pipe he held tight in his teeth,
And the smoke it encircled his head like a wreath;
He had a broad face and a little round belly,

That shook when he laughed, like a bowl full of jelly.
He was chubby and plump, a right jolly old elf,
And I laughed when I saw him, in spite of myself;
A wink of his eye and a twist of his head,
Soon gave me to know I had nothing to dread;
He spoke not a word, but went straight to his work,
And fill'd all the stockings; then turned with a jerk,
And laying his finger aside of his nose,
And giving a nod, up the chimney he rose;
He sprang to his sleigh, to his team gave a whistle,
And away they all flew like the down of a thistle.
But I heard him exclaim, ere he drove out of sight,
« Happy Christmas to all, and to all a good night ».

Moore might have preserved St. Nicholas' name in his poem, but the physical description of this « jolly old elf » is surely reminiscent of a character from northern European folklore, not of the stately saint of the Catholic Church. The event prominently takes place on Christmas Eve rather than December 5, stressing the Protestant background of the writer and his sources. The good Mr. Moore most likely learned his information from the Dutch and Germans who lived in New York and still practiced the old rituals of St. Nicholas and his Protestant successors, such as Pelznickel. In fact, it is believed that Moore modeled his portrayal of St. Nicholas on a rotund Dutch neighbor.[181] Apparently intended for private circulation only, the poem was first published anonymously on December 23, 1823, in the Troy (New York State) Sentinel newspaper.[182] An authorized

---

[181] *Ibid.*, p. 9.
[182] *Ibid.*, p. 10.

publication did not occur until 1848.[183] From then on, however, the reading of the poem became an annual delight, and its popularity aided in the establishment of a consistent pattern in the Christmas celebration among American families.

The 1848 publication applied the subtitle *Visit From Santa Claus*. The name quite obviously is a contraction of the German *Sankt Nikolaus* which – in the everyday language of the common people – sometimes loses its correct pronounciation. A Swiss dialect dictionary of 1806, for instance, lists our saint as *Samiklaus*.[184] Allowing for such local deviations, it is not too hard to imagine how the name Santa Claus came about.

Nicholas met the challenge of the New World much as he had faced the changing demands throughout the history of his cult: he adapted to his new environment. No matter how radical the transformation appears to be, there always remains some link to the original bishop of Myra. The vast distances in time and space between fourth century Byzantium and twentieth century America could not prevent the survival of his name, though in a modified form, or the aspect of generosity associated with his cult. We know that Nicholas' identity took on many disguises as a consequence of the Reformation and that his religious nature was lost to Protestants. What we are unable to ascertain due to a lack of documentation is the exact point in history

---

[183] *Ibid.*, p. 9.

[184] GEORGE H. MCKNIGHT, *St. Nicholas: His Legend and His Role in the Christmas Celebration and Other Popular Customs*, New York, G. P. Putnam's Sons 1917, p. 14.

when Nicholas attained his medieval helper or precisely when this companion supplanted the saint as distributor of gifts. Changing attitudes and customs would only transpire at the slow pace of the age, with details of these events shrouded in the mist of time. But the continuous practice of presenting presents, first on the eve of St. Nicholas Day and later on Christmas Eve, gave inspiration to Moore's poem which enlightened the nebulous traditions of the past. St. Nicholas, or Santa Claus in America, had now come to embody the gift giving characteristics of the patron of children and also the physical features of the saint's folkloric successors. When Clement Moore finally focused on Nicholas' duties on Christmas Eve, the holy man of Myra emerged synonymous with the secular Santa Claus.

The Visual Creation of Santa Claus

In the very beginning of Nicholas' cult, the remembrance of the saint depended for generations upon the effectiveness of passing along the events of his life by word of mouth. Only centuries later were those oral accounts transcribed into a literary record to be followed by translations into visual images. Much the same pattern can be detected enroute to our modern Santa Claus. From the tales and observances of the northern European immigrants sprang the poetic narrative by Clement Moore; from his lively and entertaining depiction of the Christmas visitor arose the later visual conception by Thomas Nast. Unlike earlier representations of Nicholas in art, the Santa Claus image and its popularization were mostly the work of this artist alone.

Thomas Nast was born on September 27, 1840, in the military barracks of Landau, Germany.[185] His father, a musician in a Bavarian regiment, decided to leave Germany when Thomas was six years old, and the family arrived in New York in 1846. The young Nast studied drawing in Theodore Kaufmann's studio at 442 Broadway and later entered the Academy of Design on 13th Street. With this background, Thomas Nast grew into America's greatest political cartoonist. His drawings ranged from the criticism of slavery in the South to the exposure of political corruption in New York, and at first glance he may not seem the type of artist who would be interested in the non-political subject of St. Nicholas. But Nast was not a one-sided man. During his career he published more than 3000 drawings, most of which appeared in *Harper's Weekly* between 1862 and 1885.[186] The wide distribution of this magazine made it a powerful medium, one that afforded Nast a platform from which he reached an influential audience. A noteworthy fact, for it was for the December issues of *Harper's* that Nast contributed his Christmas cartoons. Until the 1880's they were printed from wood-block engravings; then this technique was replaced by a photochemical process.[187] His drawings usually covered a

---

185 ALBERT BIGELOW PAINE, *Th. Nast: His Period and His Pictures*, Gloucester, Mass., Peter Smith 1967, p. 5.

186 MORTON KELLER, *The Art and Politics of Thomas Nast*, New York, Oxford University Press 1968, p. VII.

187 PAINE, p. 441.

full size magazine page in detailed, realistic, eye-catching compositions. The artist's outstanding ability to grasp and express an idea was fully implemented when he created a Santa Claus who personified the merry spirit of Christmas.

Although the best, Nast was not the first American artist who brought Moore's Christmas figure to life. Theodore C. Boyd, an engraver, illustrated the earliest authorized publication of Clement Moore's poem [188] in a pamphlet, where the illustrations only measured approximately 3 inches × 3 inches. Boyd's *St. Nicholas*, as he is about to step into the chimney, wearing buckled shoes, knee breeches, a vest, and a three-quarter length coat, could be taken for a figure from the eighteenth century (Fig. 55). This small Santa Claus, though still interesting from a historical point of view, is really quite a simple drawing which lacks the force of Moore's memorable, jolly character.

Thomas Nast, on the other hand, drew more complex compositions in his masterful renditions of the Christmas visitor. One of his first Santa Claus pictures, published in the Christmas edition of *Harper's* in 1863,[189] was *Christmas in Camp* (Fig. 56). Composed during the Civil War, Santa Claus is shown surrounded by soldiers as he pays a visit to a Union Army camp. The patriotic Santa, dressed in Stars and Stripes, mirrors Nast's political beliefs as a Unionist, but his work must have struck a cord with every soldier, no matter what his political persuasion, who yearned

---

[188] Clement C. Moore, *A Visit From St. Nicholas*, with original cuts, designed and engraved by Boyd, New York, Henry M. Onderdonk 1848.

[189] Paine, p. 84.

Fig. 55. - THEODORE C. BOYD: *St. Nicholas on Christmas Eve.* Illustration from first authorized publication of Clement Moore's *A Visit From St. Nicholas*, 1848.

Fig. 56. - THOMAS NAST: *Christmas in Camp.* Cartoon, originally published in *Harper's Weekly*, New York, January 3, 1863.

for home at this special time of the year. At least one emotional response was recorded in a letter written by a Union colonel, who could not hold back the tears when he saw the drawing. « It was only a picture », he wrote, « but I could not help it ».[190]

Yet, Santa Claus is known to be more familiar with the world of children than the world of soldiers. Nast's *Merry Christmas* (Fig. 57), where children happily climb Santa's lap, is a scene still enacted today across the land, and the curiosity and anticipation of young boys and girls on Christmas Day is nicely captured in *A Christmas Box* (Fig. 58). The children in Nast's compositions evidently belong to his own nineteenth century middle-class society; they are healthy, carefree youngsters.

In the art of Europe we frequently observed St. Nicholas as a spiritual intercessor between the worshipper and the heavenly realm above. Now, in the modern age of technology, his means of communication have drastically changed, as « *Hello*! *Little One*! » (Fig. 59) so charmingly illustrates. Alexander Graham Bell's recent invention proves convenient for Santa Claus as he receives requests for games and toys. Once all wishes are fulfilled and their deliveries completed, Clement Moore's last line from his poem finds a joyous, visual expression in Nast's *Merry Christmas to All, and to All a Good Night* (Fig. 60). The drawing brings to mind St. Nicholas' gravity defying feats as he saves Adeodatus (Fig. 16) or rescues a ship in distress (Fig. 44), but here the situation is much less perilous. A

---

[190] *Ibid.*, p. 84.

Fig. 57. - THOMAS NAST: *Merry Christmas.* Cartoon, originally published in *Harper's Weekly*, New York, January 4, 1879.

Fig. 58. - THOMAS NAST: *Christmas Box*. Cartoon, originally published in *Harper's Weekly*. New York, December 26, 1885.

jovial Santa Claus flies away, above a sleepy, picturesque town, and bids farewell until the next year.

Moore's portrayal of the jolly old gentleman is perhaps best caught in Nast's wonderful drawing entitled *Merry Old Santa Claus* (Fig. 61). This marvelously detailed study reveals a potbellied Santa with a smiling, broad face and a long, white beard, who contentedly holds his pipe and carries gifts for the little ones. He makes indeed a striking Christmas symbol of lasting impression. This nineteenth century Santa Claus truly forms a compelling contrast to the aesthetic St. Nicholas of the Middle Ages, and to dispel any doubt that the new creation was born from the old, Nast offers his drawing for Christmas 1882, *The Shrine of St. Nicholas – « We Are All Good Children »* (Fig. 62). In this work, Santa Claus and the saint are obviously interchangeable, for the Santa Claus figure sits on a box clearly marked St. Nicholas. The two may differ from each other in physical appearance, but they are very much of the same magnanimous spirit when it comes to rewarding all good children.

The immediate source for Nast's Santa Claus character was, without question, the poem by Clement Moore, although the artist's childhood in Germany probably introduced him to the traditions of Pelznickel or one of the other St. Nicholas replacements. In 1860, when Nast returned to Europe as an illustrator to join Garibaldi's conquering campaign in Sicily and the Italian mainland,[191] he again had ample opportunity to study the art of the continent. After the campaign, he embarked on a journey to

---

191 *Ibid.*, p. 51.

g. 59. - THOMAS NAST: « *Hello! Little One*! ». Cartoon, originally published in *Harper's Weekly*, New York, December 20, 1884.

Fig. 60. - THOMAS NAST: *Merry Christmas to All, and to All a Good Night.* Cartoon, originally published in *Harper's Weekly*, New York, c. 1864-84.

London, which included a stopover at his birthplace in Germany. Though it is unlikely that he was affected by any St. Nicholas representations he may have seen there, we do find a certain northern robustness in the facial structure of Santa Claus.

Notwithstanding Moore's influence on Nast, the heritage of the Santa Claus image lay already in some of the faces which represented the bishop of Myra in Northern art. A close-up of St. Nicholas' face, taken from a stained glass window in the church of Maria am Gestade, in Vienna,[192] depicts a distinct likeness to Santa Claus (Fig. 63). This work dates from about 1390,[193] and – appropriately enough – the detail comes from *St. Nicholas and the Three Destitute Maidens.* The stunning transition caused by the Reformation is evident in a drawing of *St. Nicholas As a Forest Spirit* (Fig. 64) by Jost Amman (1539-1591), dated 1588, and now located in the Louvre.[194] Jost Amman was an artist from Zürich who worked in Nürnberg, and his drawing reflects the changing Protestant concept of Nicholas from the miracle working saint to, in this particular case, a *Waldgeist*, or spirit of the forest. But even the wild looking costume does not hide the facial resemblance to our modern Santa Claus. I have included these two works, not to illustrate any possible direct influence on Nast but merely to demonstrate the tradition on which his cartoons are based.

---

192 Ena Frodl-Kraft, *Corpus Vitrearum Medii Aevi. Die Mittelalterlichen Glasgemälde in Wien*, Österreich Band I, Wien, Graz-Wien-Köln, Herman Böhlaus 1962, pp. 102-103.

193 *Ibid.*, p. 103.

194 Sigrid Metken, *Sankt Nikolaus in Kunst und Verbrauch*, Duisburg, Carl Lange 1966, pp. 60-61.

Fig. 61. - THOMAS NAST: *Merry Old Santa Claus.* Cartoon, originally published in *Harper's Weekly*, New York, January 1, 1881.

g. 62. - THOMAS NAST: *The Shrine of St. Nicholas – « We Are All Good hildren »*. Cartoon, originally published in *Harper's Weekly*, New York 1882.

Ironically, these traditions came to a full circle by 1880, when Nast's Christmas drawings were published in London papers.[195]

The long pictorial process toward Santa Claus started with Protestant conceptions, such as the one by Amman. Nast, probably unaware of these artistic works, drew upon his childhood images and Clement Moore's figure: « dressed all in fur from his head to his foot ... his cheeks were like roses, his nose like a cherry ... and the beard of his chin was as white as the snow; the stump of a pipe he held tight in his teeth ... he had a broad face and a little round belly ». From this description, Nast created, with variations, the visual « jolly old elf » we call Santa Claus, and who is none other than a secularized St. Nicholas.

---

195 PAINE, pp. 441-442.

Fig. 63. - Vienna, Maria am Gestade: *St. Nicholas and the Three Destitute Maidens.* Detail of St. Nicholas Stained glass window, south choir, c. 1390.

Fig. 64. - JOST AMMAN: *St. Nicholas As a Forest Spirit*, Paris, Louvre. Drawing 1588.

CONCLUSION

Today, St. Nicholas wears two hats, a bishop's mitre and a fur cap, and both with equal success. No doubt, the serious side of his dual personality stimulated the greater works of art. While both sides of his character owe a debt to writers as well as to artists, it is due to the wealth of imaginative iconography of the latter that we are left with the impression of a ubiquitous figure. But these creations alone cannot account for the saint's enduring popularity. From his modest beginning in Byzantium, he left neither philosophic writings nor fiery sermons; instead, he attracted followers from all walks of life for over 1,500 years by sheer dedication to those who suffered poverty, injustice or danger.

An irresistible force seemed to propel the cult of St. Nicholas across all Christian lands, with its survival mainly dependent on its ability to grow through the invention of new legends. Moreover, the cult's adaptability was able to overcome changes as radical as the one wrought by the Reformation. At first, the idea of replacing the holy man with a figure devoid of religion may have been fragmented and localized in Germany, but the fame of Clement Moore's poem and Thomas Nast's cartoons resulted in a more universal creation for the English speaking world. Though Christ remains the center of religious worship on Christmas, the non-religious celebration of his birth, at least in America, is now dominated by Santa Claus.

We have seen from the earliest years of his cult how St. Nicholas and his miracles appealed to a wide audience; age, nationality and high or humble station in life were no obstacles to participation in the saint's movement. To many he was the great resource in emergency. Yet, to learn the bishop's true, everlasting and universal attraction, we must take away all the miracles attributed to him. We are then left with two significant events: the giving away of his wealth to the three poor maidens and the rescue from execution of three innocent men, witnessed by the *Stratelates.* These deeds did not require any miraculous interventions but charity and a sense of justice. When seen in this light, the pious bishop of Myra is truly a provider for the needy and a protector of the innocent. These most human qualities, so well embodied in St. Nicholas, make him, so I believe, a man for all ages, including the twenty-first century.

BIBLIOGRAPHY

ALBRECHT OTTO E., *Four Latin Plays of St. Nicholas from the 12th Century Fleury Play-Book: Text and Commentary, with a Study of the Music of the Plays, and of the Sources and Iconography of the Legends*, Philadelphia, University of Pennsylvania Press 1935.

ALLEN J. ROMILLY, *Fonts of the Winchester Type*, « Journal of The British Archaeological Association », V, 50, 1894: 17-27.

ANRICH GUSTAV, *Hagios Nikolaos, der heilige Nikolaos in der griechischen Kirche*, 2 vols., Leipzig, B. G. Teubner 1913-1917.

BAKER JOHN, *English Stained Glass.* Introduction by Herbert Read, London, Thames and Hudson 1960.

BATTISTI EUGENIO; MAIURI AMEDEO; VENTURI LIONELLO, *Painting in Italy. From the Origins to the Thirtheenth Century.* Translated by James Emmons, Geneva, Skira 1959.

BIRCH W. DE GRAY, *The Legendary Life of St. Nicholas*, « The Journal of the British Archaeological Association », V, 42, 1886: 185-204; V, 44 1888: 222-234.

COLE BRUCE, *Agnolo Gaddi*, Oxford, Oxford University Press 1977.

Crowe sir Joseph A.; Cavalcaselle G. B., *A New History of Painting in Italy.* Edited by E. Hutton, 3 vols., London, Dent 1908-09.

Cust Lionel; Horn Herbert, *Quaratesi Altarpiece*, « Burlington Magazine », V, 6, 1905: 470-473.

Demus Otto, *Byzantine Art and the West*, New York, New York University Press 1970.

Gayley Charles Mills, *Plays of Our Forefathers, and Some of the Traditions upon Which They Were Founded*, New York, Duffield and Co. 1907.

Gerhard H. P., *The World of Icons*, New York, Harper and Row 1971.

Hood William; Hope Charles, *Titian's Vatican Altarpiece and the Pictures Underneath*, « Art Bulletin », V, LIX, 1977: 534-555.

Ikonen-Museum, *Kunstsammlungen der Stadt Recklinghausen*, Recklinghausen, Aurel Bongers 1968.

Jacobus de Voragine, *The Golden Legend.* Translated by Granger Ryan and Helmut Ripperger, New York, Arno Press 1969.

Kaftal George, *Iconography of the Saints in Central and South Italian Schools of Painting*, Florence, Sansoni 1965.

— *Iconography of the Saints in Tuscan Painting*, Florence, Sansoni 1952.

Keller Morton, *The Art and Politics of Thomas Nast*, New York, Oxford University Press 1968.

Kitzinger Ernst, *Late Classical and Mediaeval Studies in Honor of Albert Mathias Friend, Jr. On Some Icons of the VII Century*, Princeton, Princeton University Press 1955.

Krummer-Schroth Ingeborg, *Glasmalereien aus dem Freiburger Münster*, Freiburg im Breisgau, Rombach 1967.

LAZAREV V. N., *Novgorodian Icon-Painting*. Translated by L. N. Feonov, Moscow, Edition « Iskusstvo » 1969.

MÂLE EMILE, *Religious Art in France, XIII Century. A Study in Mediaeval Iconography and Its Sources of Inspiration*. Translated by David Buxton, London, Ernest Benn 1960.

— *The Early Churches of Rome*. Translated by David Buxton, London, Ernest Benn 1960.

MARTIN ARTHUR; CAHIER CHARLES, *Monographie de la cathedrale de Bourges*, 2 vols., Paris, M. Poussielgue-Rusand 1841-1844.

MCKNIGHT GEORGE H., *St. Nicholas: His Legend and His Role in the Christmas Celebration and Other Popular Customs*, New York, G. P. Putnam's Sons 1917.

MEISEN KARL, *Nikolauskult und Nikolausbrauch im Abendlande. Eine kultgeographisch-volkskundliche Untersuchung*, Düsseldorf, L. Schwann 1931. New Edition: Düsseldorf, Schwann-Bagel 1981.

MEISS MILLARD, *French Painting in the Time of Jean de Berry. The Boucicaut Master*, London, Phaidon 1968.

MEISS MILLARD; BEATSON ELIZABETH H., *The Belles Heures of Jean, Duke of Berry*, New York, George Braziller 1974.

MOORE CLEMENT C., *A Visit From St. Nicholas. Facsimiles of the Earliest Printed Newspaper and Pamphlet Versions and a Halograph Manuscript with a Commentary by Clifton Fadiman*, New York, Giniger 1967.

NAST THOMAS, *Thomas Nast's Christmas Drawings for the Human Race*, New York, Harper and Brothers 1890.

OLSUFIEV YOORI A., *The Development of Russian Icon Painting From the 12th to the 19th Century*, « Art Bulletin », V, 12, Dec. 1930: 346-373.

PAINE ALBERT BIGELOW, *Th. Nast: His Period and His Pictures*, Gloucester, Peter Smith 1967.

PAPAIOANNOU KOSTAS, *Byzantine and Russian Painting.* Translated by Janet Sondheimer, New York, Funk and Wagnalls 1965.

PIERCE CATHERINE W., *Francesco da Gentile da Fabriano*, « American Journal of Archaeology », V, 25, Concord 1931: 376-386.

POPE-HENNESSY JOHN, *Fra Angelico*, New York, Cornell University Press 1974.

PRIOR EDWARD S.; GARDNER ARTHUR, *An Account of Medieval Figure-Sculpture in England*, 2 vols., Cambridge, Cambridge University Press 1912.

ROWLEY GEORGE, *Ambrogio Lorenzetti*, 2 vols., Princeton, Princeton University Press 1958.

— *Late Classical and Mediaeval Studies in Honor of Albert Mathias Friend, Jr. The S. Niccolò Narratives by Ambrogio Lorenzetti*, Princeton, Princeton University Press 1955.

SIRÉN OSVALD, *Giotto and Some of His Followers*, 2 vols., Cambridge, Harvard University Press 1917.

SMIRNOVA E.; YAMSHCHIKOV S., *Old Russian Painting. Latest Discoveries. Obonezhye Painting 14th-18th Centuries*, Leningrad, Aurora Art Publisher 1974.

SOTIRIOU M. et G., *Icones du Mont Sinai*, 2 vols., Athènes, Collection de l'Institut Français d'Athènes 1956-1958.

STEPHENS WILLIAM EDWARD WOOD, *The History of the Cathedral Font, Winchester*, « Journal of the British Archaeological Association », V, 50, 1894: 6-16.

SUIDA WILHELM, *Two Unpublished Paintings by Gentile da Fabriano*, « Art Quarterly », V, 3, 1940: 348-352.

Talbot Rice David, *Byzantine Painting. The Last Phase*, New York, The Dial Press 1968.

Talbot Rice David; Talbot Rice Tamara, *Icons and Their History*, New York, The Overlook Press 1974.

Talbot Rice Tamara, *Russian Icons*, New York, Marlboro Books 1963.

Toesca Pietro, *Florentine Painting of the Trecento*, New York, Harcourt, Brace 1929.

Vasari Giorgio, *Lives of Seventy of the Most Eminent Painters, Sculptors and Architects.* Edited and annotated by E. H. and E. W. Blashfield and A. A. Hopkins, V, 2, New York, Charles Scribner's Sons 1911.

Ware Timothy, *The Orthodox Church*, London, Penguin Books 1963.

Weitzmann Kurt, *Studies in Classical and Byzantine Manuscript Illumination.* Edited by Herbert L. Kessler, Chicago, University of Chicago Press 1971.

— *The Icon. Holy Images-Sixth to Fourteenth Century*, New York, G. Braziller 1978.

— *The Monastery of Saint Catherine at Mount Sinai. The Icons.* V. 1: *From the Sixth to the Tenth Century*, Princeton, Princeton University Press 1976.

Weitzmann Kurt; Chatzidakis M.; Miatev K., Radojcic S., *A Treasury of Sixth to Seventeenth Century Icons From the Sinai Peninsula, Greece, Bulgaria and Yugoslavia*, New York, Harry N. Abrams 1966.

Wilpert Joseph, *Die Römischen Mosaiken und Malereien der kirchlichen Bauten vom IV. bis XIII. Jahrhundert*, V, 4, Freiburg im Breisgau, Herder & C. GMBH 1924.

LIST OF ILLUSTRATIONS

Fig. 9. - Recklinghausen, Ikonenmuseum: *St. Nicholas.* Icon from Moscow, beginning of 16th cetnury.

Fig. 10. - Recklinghausen, Ikonenmuseum: *St. Nicholas.* Biographical icon from Novgorod, beginning of 16th century.

Fig. 11. - Recklinghausen, Ikonenmuseum: *St. Nicholas Saves a Ship in a Storm*. Detail of Fig. 10.

Fig. 12. - Bari, Church of St. Nicholas: *St. Nicholas and Scenes From His Life.* Stone relief, 13th century.

Fig. 13. - Assisi, Cappella del Sacramento in the Church of San Francesco: *St. Nicholas Saves Three Men From Execution.* Fresco.

Fig. 14. - Assisi, Cappella del Sacramento in the Church of San Francesco: *St. Nicholas Forgives the Guilty Consul.* Fresco.

Fig. 15. - Assisi, Cappella del Sacramento in the Church of San Francesco: *St. Nicholas Appears in Constantine's Dream.* Fresco.

Fig. 16. - Assisi, Cappella del Sacramento in the Church of San Francesco: *St. Nicholas Saves Adeodatus From Slavery and Returns Him to His Parents.* Fresco.

Fig. 17. - Ambrogio Lorenzetti: *The Three Destitute Maidens*, Florence, Uffizi. Wing of triptych, c. 1327-32.

Fig. 18. - Ambrogio Lorenzetti: *Consecration of St. Nicholas*, Florence, Uffizi. Wing of triptych, c. 1327-32.

Fig. 19. - Ambrogio Lorenzetti: *St. Nicholas Revives a Child Strangled by the Devil*, Florence, Uffizi. Wing of triptych, c. 1327-32.

Fig. 20. - Ambrogio Lorenzetti: *The Miracle of the Corn Ships*, Florence, Uffizi. Wing of triptych, c. 1327-32.

PHOTOGRAPHIC ACKNOWLEDGEMENTS

I wish to express my thanks to all the museums whose works are represented in this book for their permission to reproduce illustrations, and to the following: Alinari for Figs. 13-24 and 29-38; J. E. Bulloz, Paris, for Fig. 43; the Bundesdenkmalamt, Wien, for Fig. 63; Mr. Alfred Lammer, London, for Figs. 51-54; the New York Public Library, Rare Books and Manuscripts Division, for Fig. 55; the New York Public Library, Print Collection, for Figs. 56-62; Rombach & Co., Freiburg im Breisgau, for Figs. 49 and 50; E. Schmidt-Ullrich, Bochum, for Figs. 9-11; Dr. Kurt Weitzman for Figs. 1-5.

INDEX

PART ONE

SAINT NICHOLAS IN BYZANTIUM

PART TWO

SAINT NICHOLAS IN ITALY

Part Three

SAINT NICHOLAS IN NORTHERN EUROPE

Part Four

SAINT NICHOLAS' TRANSFORMATION IN AMERICA